WHY AM I STILL SINGLE?

Finding the Love You Want & Deserve

GIOVANNA BURGESS GEATHERS, MA, LPC

Giovanna Burgess Geathers, LPC
Why Am I Still Single?
Finding the Love You Want & Deserve

Published by:
Giovanna Burgess Geathers, LLC Greenville, SC 29611

For Booking Information or to order copies, contact me at:
www.giovannageathers.com
giovannageathers@yahoo.com
www.facebook.com/GiovannaGeathers
@simplygiovannag on Instagram and Twitter

ISBN: 978-0-692-84651-3

Library of Congress Control Number: 2017903521

Printed in the United States of America
10 9 8 7 6 5 4 3 2 1

Note: This book is intended for use as an informational guide
only. The reader assumes all responsibility for the
consequences of any actions taken based on the information
presented in this book. Although the author and publisher

Dedication

My Mother
Mrs. Corrine Collins Burgess
June 12, 1936- February 5, 2016
"The strongest woman I have ever known"

     I proudly dedicate this book to my mother, the woman who gave me life and taught me to live, Mrs. Corrine Collins Burgess. My mother was born in the 1930's, the second to last child in a family of nine. My grandparents, the late Benjamin and Myrtle Moorehead Collins, raised my mother and her siblings in Anderson County and later Pickens County. My mother met and married my father in 1954 and they relocated to Chicago, Ill where they had my five siblings. Sadly, before my mother had the opportunity to tell my father she was pregnant with me, their sixth child, my father was accidentally shot and killed at the young age of thirty-eight. My mother eventually moved back to her hometown of Easley, SC where she single handedly raised my six siblings and me without any government assistance. My mother was strong, hardworking, and fiercely independent, all the qualities she did her best to instill in us. She loved hard, though she rarely expressed it, and she persevered through many trials and tribulations without ever giving up the fight. I know she had to be tired and weary on many days, but she rarely complained. She taught me so many values that I could not fully appreciate as a child and young adult, but these values have shaped my life as a mother, a wife, a speaker, a therapist and an author. There are not enough words to express the love and appreciation I have for her. She is the wind beneath my wings and the angel that watches over me, guiding my footsteps and helping to chart my journey. My one regret is that she is not here to witness and share in this accomplishment with me. She may not have been able to express it verbally, but it would have been there in her eyes and the meal she would have prepared for me as a celebration. Mama, thank you for giving me the courage to fight against all odds, to never stay down when I get knocked down and to overcome any obstacles that stand in my way. You were truly one of a kind and I can only pray that I am half the mother to Morgan and Jordan that you have been to me. Rest in Heaven Mama, until we meet again.

Acknowledgments

First off, I have to thank God for without Him and His love and encouragement, this book would have never been completed and shared with the world. God has pushed, pulled, led and guided me when the darkness threatened to consume and overtake me. Throughout every attack, every trial and every obstacle, His unfailing love, power and presence held me, sustained me, and kept me moving forward. God is truly my alpha and my omega!

To my children, Morgan and Jordan, I thank you both for being understanding and patient with me on all the mornings, days and evenings when mommy could not be there to read, play a game or simply hear about your day. Please know that each of you are my greatest joy and the reasons I work so hard to accomplish my dreams. I pray you will always know that with God on your side, you can do and become anything you imagine. Always dream big!

My husband, Jerome, what can I say to you? You are truly an amazing example of God's love for me and the inspiration for this whole book. You have shown me that real love is possible and good men do exist. I prayed for a husband like you and God answered in a way that I could never have dreamed. You are my rock, my biggest fan and my greatest friend. Thank you so much for all the encouragement and for believing in me when I felt like giving up.

Pastors Ron and Hope Carpenter of the Redemption World Outreach Center in Greenville, SC. I had been praying and seeking a ministry like yours when the Holy Spirit awakened me in 2014 and told me to visit Redemption. We have been there ever since! The growth that my family and I have experienced under your teaching is immeasurable. I have such a deeper, more intimate relationship with Christ, my husband and myself because of you. Thank you.

My sisters, Caryn and Tonya Burgess, my aunt Thelma Kirksey Perkins, and my nieces, Tasheka and LaToya McDowell, thank you all for keeping me encouraged and supporting me in everything I do.

To my other family members (especially Shane & Vivica Burgess, Tim Sitton, and Seanie Williams), my friends, clients, followers, colleagues and supporters, I thank you all from the bottom of my heart for sharing my social media posts, attending my events and for believing in me. While I cannot personally thank everyone by name, please know that you are on my mind and in my heart.

A special thank you to my recently departed brother, Tommy Ricardo Burgess, my baby brother, Juan Burgess, my parents, the late James Thomas and Corrine Collins Burgess, and my grandmother Cordelia Rosemond Burgess Kirksey. I know you are all smiling down on me from Heaven.

To my lifelong friends, Christy Fuller, TaSonya Hughes, Tonya Knox and Lisa White, thank you for always letting me dream out loud and cry on your shoulders. You ladies love me unconditionally and I cannot thank you enough for always letting me be me.

My in-laws, The Geathers family, thank you for always supporting me and my family.

To my girl, Elterrice, "El", Westfield, for assisting me with all of my legal questions, concerns and disclaimers as well as giving me encouragement and motivation. You are such an amazing person to have in my corner and I thank God for you.

My dream team Joycelin Allgood, Audrey "Tika" Clausell, Pamela Almond Hope, Juanita Jones, Gina Lotharpe, Tonya Mayes, and Tonya Woods, thank you ladies for reading excerpts, providing feedback on the content and cover design and for always being there to pray for me and with me. You chicks rock!

My mentor, Stan Davis, for encouraging me to walk in my own sunshine; my licensing supervisor and mentor, Tobias Schreiber, and my therapist, Frederike Wilday, thank you all for helping me hold it in the road! Also, thank you to Jack Surrett for writing my first recommendation!

To my gorgeous friend and cover model, Charmagne Cohens, my make-up artist, April Byrd, and my photographer, Kesha Cureton, thank you for helping bring my vision for the book cover to life!

To the readers, thank you for supporting me and buying this book. I pray that your lives and your relationships will be forever changed in a loving, positive way after this experience.

Finally, to all the broken relationships from my past. Thank you for all the life lessons and for teaching me what love isn't so I could better appreciate what true love is.

If success and wealth could be measured by the people in your life, then I am truly the wealthiest, most successful woman in the world!

Table of Contents

Introduction

Why am I still single was the question I asked myself in 2009 after a study was conducted by two researchers from Yale University which reported that 42% of professional Black women have never been married and may never get married. I still remember the first time I heard that statistic. I cringed inwardly as I wondered whether this statistic was accurate, and more importantly, did it include me? At the time, I and several of my closest friends; were still single and unmarried with my fortieth birthday only two years away. I remember thinking about myself and my history of dating, as well as my friends and their history of dating. Suffice it to say, there hadn't been many proposals of marriage. In cases where there was a proposal and/or marriage, there were even more stories of abuse, infidelity, dissatisfaction, settling, and eventual divorce. So there I was listening to the radio shows and talk shows discuss this statistic that made love and the idea of happily ever after sound hopeless for me and so many other "sistas". I recall an episode of the popular sitcom "The Game" where Tasha Mack, who was dating Coach T at the time, was feeling panicked because of some relationship conflicts that she feared would lead to a split between them and keep her trapped in that category of unmarried Black women. I wondered. What was I, Tasha Mack, and so many other Black women doing "wrong" and why was this phenomenon so heavily targeted towards us? "Hadn't we been through enough already?" Let's begin with slavery and all that Black women and Black people endured such as rapes, forced servitude, whippings, beatings, torture, and even murder. Not to mention the ever-present threat of children, parents, siblings, friends, and husbands being sold away never to be seen again. Didn't we suffer enough during reconstruction and the civil rights movement when many Black women could only find work as domestics or wet nurses? Fast forward to the 80s and 90s and the drug epidemic that destroyed so many women's lives, their children's lives, and family's lives. After the drug epidemic, Black women became the leading group of people who were more likely than any other group of people to contract HIV and die from AIDS-related complications. To top all of that off, now there was a national study reporting that almost half of us have never been married and were also likely never to get married. I remember looking closely at myself. I was a successful, attractive, graduate degreed homeowner and driving a nearly new Infiniti. I had good credit, excellent credentials, and good intentions and yet when it came to love, relationships, and marriage, I was failing miserably. In fact, my relationship history had been pretty unhealthy, unfulfilling and even emotionally and verbally abusive at times. So it wasn't as if I hadn't thought about never finding Mr. Right before, I just always pushed those thoughts along with my fears to the back of my mind.

At the time this study was published in 2009, I was in a somewhat healthy relationship of two years with the father of my newborn son…still unmarried, but happy. Happy because I was finally involved with a man who I believed truly liked and loved me for me, respected me and treated me as I had always longed to be treated;

actually he treated me better. For the first time in a long time, my relationship was working. Not only were we compatible, we were also friends; but because we were still unmarried, living two hours apart and not engaged, my fears were still there because no matter how well things were going, the reality was that I was someone's baby mama. Not quite the fairytale life I had envisioned for myself; yet for the time being it was working and at least appeared to be moving in the direction of happily ever after.

During those first two years of our relationship, I learned a lot about men, about women, about love, and about me, so as I thought about what made this relationship different from my previous relationships, I asked myself, "What had I finally learned that was changing the course of love in my life and how could I capture this lesson and share it with other women?" I began to read and gather information so that I could better understand how I and many other women like me had arrived at a place where we felt we weren't seen as desirable mates and wives. A place that continually showed us we weren't good enough, weren't pretty enough, weren't submissive enough or supportive enough. A place that said we were okay as girlfriends, "live-ins", baby mamas, and wifey (wife-like). Even more so, when did we as women start believing these lies? When did we decide it was acceptable to simply live with someone for years and not expect and demand more? When did we begin to settle for playing house instead of building homes? I thought about the number of women I had heard actually reject and denounce the idea of love and marriage, then go on to have two or more children by the same man or several different men. These same women would frequently remain in relationships and situations that continually demeaned them and not only destroyed their self-esteem, but also denigrated their womanhood. Again I asked myself, "When did Black women decide that we were somehow less than, inferior, and unworthy of true love?" When did we choose to allow ourselves to become someone's side chick and glorify it? How did we begin to assume the role of man and woman in our own lives and in our children's lives so much so that when a real man shows up, we are unsure of how to allow him to be the man? When did we choose to willingly enter into and remain in relationships where we are abused verbally, physically, emotionally, mentally, and sexually? Where did we get so far off course, give away our power and settle for an existence that says that half of anything is better than all of nothing? Now don't get me wrong, I fully understand that not all women desire to be married and this book was not written to tell every Black woman they need to get married, have to get married, should get married, that the goal in life is to be married, nor that they are somehow less than if they do not get married. I respect that marriage is not for everyone, and some women are perfectly fine in their singleness; however, this book was written for the women who do desire a healthy, loving relationship and marriage and for the daughters, mothers, sisters and sistas, aunts, nieces, cousins, friends, and all the other pretty brown girls around the world who need to be reminded of who they are and what they deserve in love and in life. I wrote it for the countless women who are still searching for Mr.

Right and are close to giving up on happily ever after. I wrote it for my mother, the wisest and strongest woman I have ever known. A woman who married the love of her life, my father, only to lose him way too early in her life, forcing her into single motherhood to care for and raise seven small children, including me. I wrote it for my daughter who is blessed to be growing up in the presence of her father, my husband, who shows her daily what true love, respect, admiration, and commitment looks like and feels like so that she will always know her worth, her value and her virtue and will not have to seek it outside of herself. Finally, I wrote it for me, a woman who grew up without a father and who struggled with low self-esteem and low self-worth for much of my life. A woman who desperately sought love in all the wrong places in my need for external validation, approval, and acceptance only to finally discover that the truth was in me all along. As it is also in you.

My prayer is that this book will provide valuable information, insight, and understanding for Black women in regards to our relationships with men and with ourselves. Even though the inspiration to write this book came from an article about the Black woman's search for happily ever after, my hope is that every woman reading this book will come to discover and embrace her true worth, value, and virtue regardless of her relationship status, financial status, environment, race, ethnicity, background, level of education, sexual orientation, lifestyle or past experiences.

Why Am I Still Single is not a how-to guide (the workbook will come later); instead, it is a practical in-depth look at some of the underlying and overlying factors I feel have contributed to the phenomena of unmarried Black women and what I feel are some of the reasons, origins, explanations, and myths surrounding Black women in general as well as in the context of love, relationships, and marriage. I will include current data that speaks to the growing number of single parent homes in the Black community and historical data such as slavery, discrimination, and drugs and their effects on our relationships and families. I will also include present and future trends that seem to be moving us even farther away from healthy marriages and families. I will address family of origin issues such as abandonment, rejection, absentee fathers, sexual abuse, and domestic violence; issues that may have occurred in childhood but continue to impact and shape women as adults. I will identify and explore unhealthy relationship patterns and share insights on how to break them as well as ways to overcome trust issues, emotional baggage, and more. Together, we will look at self-esteem and self-love to truly understand what it means to like yourself and love yourself and the role this plays in our relationships with ourselves and with others. We will define and identify the differences between sex and intimacy and discuss casual sex and its effects on women from both a practical and spiritual perspective. I will include some of the things I have experienced in my own search for happily ever after along with personal and professional experiences of women I have encountered who have struggled and continue to struggle to find and secure a healthy loving relationship and marriage.

Many things in my life have changed both personally and professionally since I wrote the initial introduction and outline to this book eight years ago. For starters, I am thrilled to announce that I married my "baby daddy" in a sunset ceremony overlooking the Pacific Ocean in Maui and we are happily looking forward to celebrating our fifth anniversary this year! We also added a beautiful daughter to our family in 2013. From a professional perspective, I am now a licensed psychotherapist, workshop facilitator and life coach with my own private practice where I work with a number of different individuals, families, and couples on a variety of life issues. I also speak to women, couples, families, and groups on what I have learned personally and professionally about love, relationships, and life. Unfortunately, I also lost my mother during this eight year period, but so much of her wisdom, knowledge, and advice are shared throughout this work, I am certain her presence will be felt and her voice will continue to be heard.

As you read *Why Am I Still Single*, please do so with an open mind and an open heart so that you may discover, speak, and walk in your truth; determine your worth and your value; learn to establish and maintain healthy boundaries; and become confident in expecting and asking for what you truly desire and deserve in life, in love, and in relationships. This is not a cure-all, a promise, or a guarantee of love and marriage. It is a story of the Black woman's search for love and happily ever after as she gains a deeper understanding of her relationships with men, with others, but most importantly, with herself.

Chapter 1

The Fairytale and the Land of Not So Happily Ever After

In December of 2014, while celebrating my sister's birthday in one of my favorite cities in the world, New York City, she and I went to see the Broadway production of Rodgers and Hammerstein's Cinderella starring Keke Palmer and Nene Leakes. It was my first time on Broadway, and I must admit that the play was astounding, and the entire cast gave stellar performances. To top it off, my sister and I were able to meet Nene Leakes after the show and take a quick photo.

Now, most of us are familiar with the story of Cinderella, and I have since learned that this fairytale has many versions and has been translated into different languages and cultures. Perhaps one of the most familiar versions involves a young woman named Ella whose own mother is deceased and whose father remarries a woman with two daughters. This stepmother is very cruel to Ella and forces her to cook, clean, and care for her and her two wicked stepsisters. The story goes on to include Cinderella meeting Prince Charming, attending the royal ball with the help of her fairy godmother, and of course losing the glass slipper at midnight. Then, there is the search to find the woman with the glass slipper, and finally, the story ends with the prince riding in on his white horse to rescue Cinderella, and they live happily ever after. As a child, I can remember being fascinated by the story of Cinderella and other fairy tales that involved a beautiful princess being rescued by a handsome prince on a white horse. Only when I looked around my home, my neighborhood, and my environment, I felt far from a princess, and there were no royal balls, princes on white horses, fairy Godmothers, or glass slippers. What I did see was my single mother working day in and day out to provide for my siblings and me. I saw a woman not only cooking for us, washing our clothes, and making sure we did our homework, but also arguing with the mechanics when there was car trouble, stressing over paying the bills with so little money and playing the role of mother and father to me, my sisters, and my brothers.

As I sat in the crowded theater that rainy night on Broadway, I could not help but reflect on the number of women I knew personally and professionally who were still searching for their prince charming and the land of happily ever after. I also thought of the many women I knew who had completely trashed the idea of Cinderella, prince charming, and the land of happily ever after, and chosen instead to reside in the land of just enough, not enough, never enough, and had enough. The truth is that although many women from different lands, different cultures, ethnicities, and backgrounds share the common goal of finding and engaging in a healthy, meaningful relationship, many are discovering that "happily ever after" may not exist after all… except in fairytales.

As I mentioned in the introduction, I initially became interested in this subject following a study in 2009 (that has since been debated and updated), which was released revealing that almost half of African- American women have never been married. I decided that if that number was indeed accurate, then there had to be reasons behind it and not just a shortage of "good and available Black men." I also didn't think it was as simple as Black women being unattractive, angry, gold diggers with nasty attitudes who are unable or unwilling to submit to their men. Whatever the reasons, I knew far too many women who were settling for unhappy marriages, troubled relationships, and casual sex partners while others continued to hope, pray, and search for the ineffable Mr. Right to ride in on his white horse and rescue her from a life of singleness, loneliness, and unfulfillment. When this fails to happen, countless women give up on finding Mr. Right and decide to become okay with Mr. Right Now.

For years, my friends and I were caught up in a relentless cycle of meeting guys who initially seemed to be so nice and so different from past romantic partners. We would start dating him, become intimate way too soon, overlook all the little red flags that were popping up, and eventually have to move on when those little red flags became three alarm sirens that could no longer be justified, excused or ignored. We blamed the men. We told ourselves and each other that "men are dogs" and that we just hadn't met the right one yet. We never stopped to consider or admit that we may have been contributing to the problem. We were not willing to accept responsibility for our own actions or admit that some of the issues may have been with us or within us. We were caught up in the name game and the blame game and it was so much easier to point fingers at the men than look inside ourselves in search of the truth. Perhaps our relationships could change, but for that to happen, we had to be willing to change. I am in no way insinuating that my friends and I, nor women in general, are to blame for men's actions or inactions, but what I am suggesting is that we as women have far more power than we give ourselves credit for and in having this power, we are far more responsible than we may be willing to accept and admit. Once we become aware of our power and accept the fact that we may have willingly chosen to give up that power, we become 100% responsible for our actions, our decisions, our choices, and our lives. In short, we can no longer play the victim.

Growing up, I would often hear my mother say that women were the reason men acted the way they did in relationships. I remember being furious with her thinking, "How could my mother, a woman, suggest such a thing?" Of course, I strongly argued that men acted the way they did because that is what they chose to do and women were not responsible for how they acted. I told her that there were not a lot of good men out there and women just had to keep looking until they found the right one. What I didn't understand at the time was that my mother, in her own unique way, was teaching me that we teach people how to treat us by what we put up with and what we allow, which makes us at least partly responsible. How many times had I willingly and knowingly allowed a man to disrespect me and stayed in the relationship? How often had I overlooked poor treatment knowing it was less than what I deserved just to avoid ending up single again? How many stories had I heard from my girlfriends and associates about men cheating, lying, cursing them, hitting them, and mistreating them in countless other ways? While each case may have been different and each woman no doubt had different reasons as to why she stayed, in the end the unspoken messages we were sending were loud and clear. "I am not worthy of you treating me with dignity and respect, but instead of me assuming responsibility for my own happiness and well-being, I will blame you, curse you, and hold you accountable." Some women will argue that this is not the message they intended to send and it is far from the message I wished to convey, but the reality is that my intentions did not line up with actions and my actions spoke volumes. I would make a fuss, argue, and threaten to leave if one or more undesirable behaviors did not change, only to eventually give in, remain in the relationship and bury a bit more resentment in my heart towards men. What I know now that I didn't know then is that as adults, we are responsible for our own happiness and well-being and if someone isn't treating us in a way that we feel we deserve, we have the right and the responsibility to choose how we respond. We can respond by tolerating it or we can respond by setting boundaries and limitations on what we will and will not accept. It is not our job to try and change other people. It is our job to make the changes within ourselves and the decisions for ourselves that better serve and support who we are and where we are in life. Unfortunately, because so many of us do not know our own innate worth and value, we often search for someone or something outside of ourselves to provide this for us and every time we do this, we unconsciously make the decision to give away our power. You cannot expect someone else to do for you what you are not willing to do for yourself. You can't ask and expect someone to see and know your value when you do not see it within yourself.

A couple of years ago, my sister, a friend, and I were visiting Sports One Bar in Charlotte, NC. As we stood in line waiting to order, I overheard three guys talking behind us. I paid little attention to their conversation until I heard one of them say that he was looking for a woman with low self-esteem that night. I could not believe my ears! As I turned around with my mouth open, he laughed and shrugged his shoulders as he realized I had overheard his statement. Later, when I shared that story with a male friend, he informed me that what I heard was nothing as he had friends who deliberately set out to meet women with low self-esteem and daddy issues. While this may be shocking to hear, the reality is that it is not a man's responsibility to determine your worth and your value as a woman. Love and marriage is not a fairytale, and you are not likely to be rescued from yourself and your "stuff."

In my work with couples, I often see this issue come up as we begin to discuss areas of dissatisfaction and each partner's individual views and expectations. It quickly becomes apparent that one or both of them have entered into the relationship without ever discussing these things or they have come into it with unrealistic expectations. Time and again, I see people trying to make their partners responsible for their happiness and well-being, and when their partners cannot, do not or will not live up to their expectations, they become angry and resentful and feel as if they have been wronged. I have found that a lot of people, both men and women, expect that their partners and their relationships will somehow fix their lives, make up for their troubled pasts, give them a sense of worth and value, and make them feel secure and complete. Many adult women and men are walking around with wounded little girls and little boys on the inside of them who are still crying out for the acceptance, approval, and validation that they did not receive as children. Often, these men and women still have a list of unmet emotional needs that they carry into their interpersonal relationships. When you have one or both partners still carrying childhood wounds and unmet needs entering into relationships and marriages, you will see lots of communication issues, infidelity, emotional immaturity, disrespect, frequent arguments, and even abuse.

In couple's therapy, I usually work with both partners together and separately to identify and resolve any of their individual unmet emotional needs. My goal is to help them heal their own individual wounds and accept responsibility for their own stuff so that they are bringing their best selves to the relationship instead of blaming their issues on their mates. It is essential to the health of a relationship for each partner to be willing to work on themselves to become healthy happy human beings and not place this burden of responsibility on their partners. Even good relationships involve work and unhealthy ones involve more work.

One day, shortly after I had gotten married, I found myself seated next to an older lady in the hair salon. Upon seeing my ring, she asked me when I had gotten married. After congratulating me, she informed me that she had been married almost 30 years. She went on to share some of her dos and don'ts and then she said something so simple, yet so profound, it amazed me and I have never forgotten it. She said, "It hasn't been perfect, but it's been good. And when you can say it's good even when it isn't perfect, you've got a good marriage." I remember thinking, "Wow! How amazing is that!" Since then, I have shared that simple advice with many of the couples I work with as we all sometimes have to be reminded that relationships are not perfect and people are not perfect. We all have work to do and that work begins within. If we truly desire to attract and maintain a healthy loving relationship, then we have to understand that love, relationships, and even marriage is not a fairy tale, but they also do not have to be nightmares. Knowing what to expect, knowing what you want and what you are worth as well as doing the necessary work that may be required to heal old wounds can be beneficial in helping you break negative relationship patterns and make room for what you truly desire. Let's take a closer look at what some of those things may be.

Chapter 2

Overcoming the Past

Family of Origin Issues

Thanks to trailblazers like Iyanla Vanzant and Oprah Winfrey, we are now more aware than ever before of how the presence and absence of a strong father or father figure affects little girls and little boys in their growth and development. I developed and conduct my own workshop for fatherless daughters called "Daddy's Girl." Daddy's Girl focuses on the effects that absentee fathers have on a girl's self-esteem and self-worth, her identity, her ability to trust and her interpersonal relationships. In this workshop, I include psychological as well as practical data and information to help women identify how this may be affecting them. I also share my own personal experience of not having my father present and the many unanswered questions I had growing up about my identity and myself. How I often felt like something was missing in my life and that I was different from other girls around me who had their daddies. How I grew up without a father to validate me, affirm me, and demonstrate to me how I should expect to be treated by men, what I should look for and what I should avoid. I did have four older brothers, but they were struggling themselves to discover how to become men without the example and presence of a father. So I, like many fatherless little girls like me, went through life not knowing and not accepting who I was or what I truly deserved. I remember dreaming of what it must have felt like to call someone daddy, to be able to crawl up in his lap and have him hold me and assure me of how much I was loved and valued. Someone to shield me and protect me from anything or anyone that appeared to be a threat to me. I fantasized about my father interrogating my boyfriends and promising bodily harm if they dared not treat his princess the way he treated her. I longed for him to help me move in and out of my dorm in college, to send me money, fix my car, and brag to his friends after I graduated and got my first job. I dreamed about him walking me down the aisle on my wedding day and holding his first grandchild in his arms. Sadly, I was left with only my dreams and fantasies as I muddled through my life and my relationships blindly, all the time envying those around me who had someone to call "daddy."

When my youngest sister's father would come around with extra gifts for her at Christmas, Valentine's Day, Easter, and birthdays, I remember asking myself what I had done wrong to make me different. While I was grateful for my mother and her efforts to fill this gap, there was still something yearning inside of me that wanted and needed to know my father and to experience a father's love, protection, guidance, and support. Because of this, I often felt unfulfilled and incomplete, and I attempted to fulfill these needs through my relationships. I, like so many other girls and women, looked to boys and men to tell me I was pretty, to make me feel worthy, important, special, and desirable. I was seeking validation, approval, and acceptance from them and through them. I didn't know then what I know now, that if we do not receive validation, approval, and acceptance from our fathers or our mothers while growing up, as adults we have to do that work for ourselves because even if we do happen to find these things in a relationship, if the relationship ends, we are right back to needing and seeking those things again. We may go through our whole lives never realizing that what we are searching for externally can only be found internally. As we learn to nurture and develop our own internal sense of self-acceptance, self-approval, and self-validation, we will no longer allow this to be determined by other people. When we realize, acknowledge, and develop these attributes within, we never have to worry about them being taken, diminished, removed, refused or rejected by anyone else. We can go into our relationships more complete, secure, fulfilled, and content instead of needing, lacking, yearning, and longing.

The National Fatherhood Initiative, located at www.fatherhood.org, provides statistical data and information on the positive impact of father involvement as well as the effects of father absence on poverty, maternal and child health, child abuse, incarceration, crime, teenage pregnancy, drug and alcohol abuse, education, and even childhood obesity. According to their studies, children without fathers are at a higher risk of abuse and are more likely to engage in criminal behavior and become incarcerated, exhibit aggressive behavior, live in poverty, engage in early sexual activity and become teen parents. According to 2014 data from Kids Count, 66% of African-American children reside in single parent homes, a statistic that is not broken down by gender. Other more recent data suggests that the percentage of African-American children born to single mothers is as high as 72%. These numbers do not make it clear as to whether this percentage only includes single mothers who have never been married or whether it also includes women who are single as the result of a death or divorce. Regardless of how you view it, if accurate, these numbers are staggering. However, we cannot assume that the absence of fathers is always due to a lack of concern or desire to be involved in a child's life because some absences may be the result of a divorce or separation, incarceration, or even death. In my case, my parents were married and lived together prior to my father's death, so his absence was not the result of a lack of concern or desire to be in my life. Nonetheless, the effects of his absence on my growth and development were no less impactful. As I mentioned earlier, I struggled with self-doubt, low self-esteem, and low self-worth. I also felt incomplete, inadequate, and unfulfilled for much of my life. Through my own healing, I have come to realize that a daughter's relationship with her father will closely mirror her relationships with men. I once heard it said that a father is his daughter's first love and when your first love isn't there physically and/or emotionally or he is abusive or neglectful, then little girls will often struggle not only in their interpersonal relationships, but also in relationship to themselves.

As a counseling major and licensed professional, I am very familiar with human growth and development and the roles that mothers and fathers play in our lives. According to German born developmental psychologist, Erik Erikson (1902-1994) who developed psychosocial developmental theory, people move through various stages of development beginning at birth and lasting through late adulthood. The initial stage which occurs in infancy is focused on developing trust and is highly contingent upon parents or caregivers providing stability, reliability, and consistency in care. If the care is reliable and predictable, the infant will develop a sense of trust that will be carried into their relationships with others and they will feel secure even when threatened. If the care is not stable, consistent, and reliable, or was in fact harsh, inconsistent or unpredictable, often the infant will develop a sense of mistrust and lack confidence in the world around them and their abilities. This will also be carried into their other relationships and may result in anxiety, insecurity, and trust issues. The next stage in Erikson's theory occurs between the ages of eighteen months and three years of age and is focused on toddlers developing a sense of independence and becoming more confident in their ability to survive in the world. If they are shamed, overly controlled or criticized, they are likely to develop feelings of inadequacy and low self-esteem. They may also feel shame and doubt in themselves and their abilities. The third stage which occurs between ages three and five is when children begin to assert themselves more frequently, ask lots of questions, and explore their interpersonal skills through play and interacting with others. Again, if children are overly controlled, abused, shamed or criticized or made to feel like a nuisance, they may develop feelings of guilt and lack the ability to make decisions and show initiative. Throughout these initial three stages of development, mothers, fathers, and caregivers play an important role in our growth and the development of our self-esteem, self-confidence and self-worth or the lack of it and this will impact how we engage with others and expect of others in our relationships. If we do not develop a healthy sense of self-esteem, self-worth, and self-confidence, then we may allow ourselves to engage in relationships with people who are abusive, controlling, possessive, physically and/or emotionally unavailable, dishonest, unfaithful or people who simply mistreat us because we do not know or feel we deserve better.

Another thing to consider in our early growth and development is what psychologists refer to as attachment theory and attachment styles. This basically means that the ways in which we attach to our mothers, fathers, and/or caregivers in infancy and toddlerhood will have a significant impact on how we later attach as adolescents and adults in our interpersonal relationships. According to attachment theory, we will either develop secure or insecure attachments as children and these attachments will define how we attach to friends and romantic partners. Secure attachments develop when parents positively respond to their children's physical and emotional needs consistently and reliably. When this happens, children develop confidence, security, and trust that their needs will be met. This belief positively affects how they interact and connect with others as well as their expectations from others. On the other hand, when this does not happen, children may develop insecure attachments. Insecure attachments can be avoidant, ambivalent or disorganized.

With avoidant attachments, parents or caregivers may discourage the child's ability and freedom to express their feelings and as a result, they grow into adults who have difficulty expressing their feelings. They may also have trust issues and fears of intimacy. In ambivalent attachments, parents may respond some of the time to the child's needs, but the response isn't consistent or reliable and therefore the child does not develop the security or confidence that they will always be taken care of. These children become adults who may need constant reassurance, validation and approval.

Lastly, disorganized attachments involve parents or caregivers who may be physically, mentally and/or emotionally abusive and neglectful. These children often become adults who are overly aggressive, abusive, and controlling with a pattern of unstable, unhealthy, and broken relationships.

I attended a seminar once that even suggested that the ways we attach to our parents also determines how we view and attach to God. According to the presenter, if we have secure attachments with our parents and caregivers, then we will have a secure attachment to God and we will trust Him to be there for us and protect us. If we have ambivalent attachments to parents and caregivers, we may believe that God will sometimes be there for us, but not all the time. Avoidant or disorganized attachments with our parents can lead us to perceive God as distant, cold, and uninvolved or we may even have the belief that there is no God.

While there may be other factors that shape our relationships, positively or negatively, it is safe to say that parents and caregivers have a significant impact on how children grow and develop into adulthood. Many adults who suffer from feelings of abandonment, rejection, inadequacy, unworthiness, helplessness, hopelessness, loneliness, mistrust, control, jealousy, and insecurity were physically, sexually, mentally, verbally, and emotionally wounded as children. This is certainly not an excuse or a justification for bad, irresponsible or abusive behavior, but it is something that needs to be considered as we enter and engage in relationships and marriages because these things often have lasting effects on us if they are unresolved. I have worked with numerous adults who still struggle internally and externally because of things that happened in childhood. I have seen women who cannot be intimate with their husbands because of their fears and distrust of men. I have seen men who were abusive, mean, distant, and unloving towards their partners or wives because they were demeaned, degraded, and devalued themselves as children. Wounded people often enter into relationships and marriages seeking and needing someone to fix them, heal them, complete them, validate them, approve of them or simply to make up for what they lost or never received as children. I too was one of those people.

My father died almost nine months before I was born. As a result, I grew up with lots of unmet emotional needs. Although mentally I understood that his dying was not a choice, it didn't seem to matter to the little girl who was longing for and needing him on birthdays, holidays, good days, and bad days. It didn't comfort the little girl who needed validation, affirmation, support, protection, guidance, and security. I grew up with so many internalized feelings of rejection, abandonment, mistrust, insecurity, low self-esteem, and low self-worth that I made it a point to do everything I could to hide these feelings. I over-compensated by excelling in school, running track, singing on the chorus, serving on student council, competing in the school talent show and beauty pageants. After graduating from high school and college, I moved to New York City and then Atlanta. I later earned my Master's degree in counseling, became a real estate investor, a make-up artist, and an events planner. From all outward appearances, I was successful, outgoing, and attractive. Yet on the inside, I was a broken, hurting, lost little girl inside a woman's body still longing and yearning for my daddy. I was needy, vulnerable, codependent, and wounded. Being wounded is like sending out an unconscious signal that attracts predators from every direction. I often say to my clients, sharks can smell blood in the water from miles away and if you are wounded and bleeding, a shark will find you.

Mommy Issues

Not all family of origin issues are about fathers; some women have mommy issues. It is no secret that many women were emotionally abused or wounded as children and adolescents by their mothers. Mothers who were overbearing, domineering, controlling, needy, emotionally unhealthy, and unavailable. I have worked with both children and adults whose mothers were too consumed by their relationships with men to pay attention to them or who were struggling with their own unresolved issues of childhood abuse, abandonment, rejection, addiction, depression, anxiety, and other emotional challenges. I have worked with children and adults whose mothers did not naturally have the "motherhood" gene and really did not wish to be mothers. This may include women who got pregnant too young, too soon or by someone they later grew to despise. Unfortunately, some of these women blamed their children and took their anger and frustration out on them. I have also seen daughters whose mothers were never "mothered" themselves, so they lack the knowledge, the ability or the willingness to provide their daughters with what they needed from them emotionally. I have also worked with mothers who seemed to feel pure resentment and contempt towards their daughters only to be surprised when their daughters mirrored these feelings back to them. In many instances, women may have a physical relationship with their daughters, but there is no emotional relationship between them, meaning these women have been taught to provide for their daughters' physical and material needs, but were never taught to provide for their emotional needs. Sadly, I see this all too often in the Black community with mothers who do a phenomenal job at providing for their children's physical, material, and even spiritual needs, but never learn to tend to and nurture their emotional needs. This often happens because they themselves were never shown this by their own mothers and their mothers before them, so this terrible pattern of emotional neglect continues and leaves little girls starving for attention, desperate to fit in and yearning to be "mothered." While I do understand and have seen firsthand how difficult some teenaged girls can be, I also believe that many of them are silently crying out and yearning to connect to their mothers in ways that make them feel validated, affirmed, and unconditionally loved and accepted despite their flaws and mistakes. When these emotional needs are not met, they often seek to fill them in some of the same ways they seek to fill the voids left by fathers. They look for love and acceptance from others and go into their relationships needy, lacking, and longing for someone to fill this space.

As a strong, independent little girl, I desperately needed my mother in ways I could not articulate. My mother, having been raised to be strong, independent, and not show her emotions, was unaware of how to fulfill my needs. She did a great job of providing for me physically and materially, especially as a single parent of seven children with only a high school education, but she wasn't comfortable expressing and displaying her emotions. My mother could write the words "I love you," but she could not say it. As a result, many of my emotional needs were unmet and I searched for ways to meet and fulfill them in all the wrong places. I was starving or as we like to say now, I was *thirsty*. Not only was I a fatherless daughter, but my mother was too overwhelmed and too preoccupied with trying to survive to attend to my emotional needs. As a child, I never understood this and it made me angry, but once I became an adult and began to heal, I was able to let go of this anger and discover ways to fill my own emotional needs. The great thing about life is that whatever we may not have received physically, verbally, emotionally or even spiritually as children, we can learn to provide for ourselves as adults. We can choose to spend our lives being angry and complaining about what we never received or what we feel someone owes us or we can learn to fill our own cups and meet our own emotional needs.

While our relationships in adulthood are often shaped by our personal relationships with our mothers and fathers, our views and attitudes can also be shaped by the relationships around us and the interactions we observed between those around us. I have spoken in detail about the absence of fathers and father figures, but it is also important to mention that in homes where a father was present, relationship dynamics such as domestic violence, infidelity, dishonesty, substance abuse, mental illness, or even the reversal of traditional gender roles can still negatively affect little girls and cause them to struggle with attracting and maintaining healthy relationships as adults. Children often imitate what they see and if their views on love, relationships, and marriage have been skewed by observing unhealthy interactions between the people around them, this becomes the model for their adult relationships. For example, if everyone in the family lives with their mates without ever being married, this creates a belief that marriage is irrelevant and unnecessary. If children observe their mothers or fathers dating outside of the marriage and/or having outside children, this will often affect how they view monogamy and fidelity in marriage and relationships. If there is constant physical violence and relationship drama, this too forms the basis for the relationships children will emulate as adults. How many little girls who grew up with physically abusive fathers have ended up marrying or dating physically abusive men? No matter how many times they may vow not to repeat their parents' mistakes, the reality is that children do what they see and what they are taught in word, deed, and action.

Rape and Sexual Abuse

Finally, let's explore how childhood issues such as sexual assault and rape affect our social and emotional development and interpersonal relationships as adults. According to statistics from RAINN.org, (Rape, Abuse & Incest National Network), the nation's largest anti-sexual violence organization, a child is sexually assaulted every eight minutes in this country. Thirty-four percent of those children are under the age of twelve and sixty-six percent of those victims are between the ages of 12-17. Keep in mind, these are "reported" cases of sexual assault. The majority of victims of sexual assault do not disclose, and of those that do disclose, many of them do not report it to the authorities. Fewer still are the number of perpetrators who are actually brought to justice.

Approximately forty percent of the adults in my private practice who are struggling with depression, anxiety, low self-esteem, current and past drug abuse or alcoholism, self-hatred, perfectionism, self-sabotage, sexual dysfunction, etc., are victims of childhood sexual abuse and/or rape. Many of them have carried the secrecy and shame of their abuse since childhood and are now in their thirties, forties, fifties, and sixties. Some of them have never disclosed the abuse to anyone until they share it with me and I witness firsthand the effects their abuse has on them as individuals and the toll it has taken on their families and relationships. When I work with couples where the wife has been abused, I often try to educate the husbands on the effects of abuse so that they do not continue to feel rejected and offended if their wives refuse sex and emotional intimacy. For people who have never experienced sexual abuse and rape, it can be difficult to understand and explain. Women who are adult survivors of childhood abuse often struggle in their interpersonal relationships with men, especially if the perpetrator was a male. They may have trust issues and other insecurities, poor boundaries, low self-esteem, and a negative self-image. I too am an adult survivor of childhood sexual abuse and rape, although I choose to call myself an overcomer rather than a survivor. In my opinion, surviving simply means you lived through it, not necessarily that you have overcome it. Please allow me to share my story.

My sexual abuse included a series of random events that occurred between the ages of eight and thirteen. It involved two close family members and my mother's long term boyfriend who I considered to be my stepfather. At the time, I had no knowledge or experience with sexual matters, so when strange things began happening to me, I was initially unsure of what was really going on. Instinctively, I knew it was wrong, but I couldn't understand why it was happening to me. "I am a good girl", I told myself. I did what my mother told me to do. I made good grades. I went to church and I prayed. Like many abused children, I blamed myself. I figured that if bad things were happening to me, then it must mean that I was bad. Self-blame is one of the hardest things to overcome because it leads you to constantly judge yourself, criticize your actions, doubt yourself, punish yourself, and even hate yourself at some level. It also leads to poor self-image, low self-esteem, self-worth, and perfectionism. I have learned that perfectionism is one of the ways children and adults try to overcompensate for inner feelings of shame and inadequacy. Perfectionism comes from a false belief that if you become perfect, then bad things will not happen to you and you will be loved and accepted. I struggled with all those things and I tried to be perfect, yet bad things continued to happen. When I was a freshman in college, I allowed a guy I had met through my next door neighbor to wait for her in my room. Sadly, he ended up raping me that same night because "he was attracted to me". Needless to say, I refused to report it to the campus police because I did not want to be judged for allowing him into my room. A couple of years ago, I located him on Facebook and was finally able to confront him about what happened. I had actually already forgiven him, but the fact that he apologized gave me an even greater sense of peace.

Since then, I have also chosen to confront my other three perpetrators, my two cousins who are still living and my stepfather who is now deceased. (Yes, you can confront the dead!) The reasons I chose to confront them was not only to acknowledge the wrong that was done to me, but also to reclaim my power and freedom. I am proud to say that I can actually be around the two family members now without feeling the urge to either run away or spit on them. (That is one of the differences between surviving and overcoming). I honestly no longer feel like a victim of their actions and I have been able to undo years of internal emotional and psychological damage. I have also chosen to use my experiences as a way of helping other abuse victims not only overcome their abuse, but also find peace with themselves and within themselves.

If you are a victim of childhood sexual abuse or rape, you do not have to continue to suffer in silence. Organizations like RAINN and therapists like myself are readily available to assist you in understanding that your abuse was not your fault and you no longer have to live with the secrets, the burdens, the shame, and the pain. You also do not have to continue to allow it to destroy your relationships with others and with yourself. You only have one life and this is not a dress rehearsal. You can take back your power, overcome your abuse, and reclaim your freedom so that you can engage in healthy happy relationships with others and with yourself! I am a living testimony that with God, your faith and determination, you can overcome your abusive past and learn healthier ways of dating, mating, and relating.

Chapter 3

Let's Talk About Sex

I could not write a book about women and relationships without addressing the areas of sex and intimacy, a subject that we have become increasingly casual about in today's society. A subject that can have lasting effects on us physically, emotionally, mentally, and spiritually. Let's first define sex and intimacy so that we can have a thorough understanding of the two and the differences between them. Wikipedia defines sex, also referred to as sexual intercourse, sexual activity or coitus as the physical act of two individuals engaging in sexual contact that involves penetration of the vagina with the penis for physical or emotional pleasure and bonding. This also includes other forms of intercourse such as penetrative oral and anal sex which are common to both heterosexual and same-sex relationships. Non-penetrative sexual acts, i.e. masturbation is called "outercourse." According to Wikipedia, intimacy refers to the "feeling" of being close to someone with a sense of belonging. It is a familiar, close connection that comes from the bond that is formed through knowledge and experience. In short, intimacy is not casual sex nor does it result from rushing into sex the first night, the first week or the first month. Intimacy takes time to develop and genuine intimacy requires open dialogue, transparency, vulnerability, and reciprocity. This basically means that true intimacy is built on honesty, give and take by both partners, open discussion, and the courage and willingness to let down emotional walls.

I am not quite sure when I learned the difference between sex and intimacy or even knew that there was a difference. One thing I am certain of is that not knowing the difference and engaging in one while really desiring the other can be detrimental, disappointing, and heartbreaking. What I mean is that many single women who regularly engage in sexual intercourse really desire intimacy, but by not knowing and understanding the difference, they settle for sex. I strongly believe that most women really want to feel loved, cared for, protected, and respected, but often compromise themselves and settle for sex in the hopes that it will automatically lead to intimacy when many times it is just sex. When their needs and expectations of intimacy are unrealized and unmet, they are then left feeling used, disrespected, unfulfilled, empty, rejected, abandoned, and even worthless. Far too many women knowingly and unknowingly give away their power by becoming sexually involved way too early with partners they barely know simply because they are inwardly craving and needing to feel wanted, loved, respected, and desired. They deny their worth and sacrifice their virtue in order to be liked, accepted, appreciated, valued, and "attached." In the previous chapter, I discussed how we form secure, ambivalent, anxious or avoidant attachments with our parents and caregivers and how poor or insecure attachments can lead to the development of attachment issues in our interpersonal relationships. Attachment issues can cause us to be needy, clingy, codependent, insecure, passive, aggressive, people pleasing, possessive, controlling, untrusting, abusive and/or abused. Women who grew up feeling abandoned, rejected, and neglected, may have overwhelming fears of being alone. These fears may cause them to rush into romantic and sexual relationships and overlook warning signs of dishonesty, disrespect, infidelity, abuse, control, or commitment issues to avoid being alone. Attachment issues can also cause women to remain in these unhealthy relationships because it feels "safer" to be attached to someone even if that someone is unhealthy and/or abusive. Women with attachment issues may also have poor boundaries and fail to set limits and expectations in their relationships. In short, these are often women who knowingly share their partners with other people and either choose to "not know" or choose to live with it and accept it. This also includes women who, not knowing their true worth or value, have chosen to be the other woman in a man's life in exchange for material items, sexual pleasure, or promises of a future relationship.

In this chapter on sex and intimacy, I want to look at each of them in regards to their practical and spiritual implications. Practical implications include physical, emotional, mental, and even social aspects while spiritual involves a person's faith and belief system.

It was around 1995 when I, along with a group of friends, first saw Juanita Bynum's video, "No More Sheets" and heard for the first time some really strong suggestions about sex, especially as it related to relationships and spirituality. At the time, I was around 23 years old, sexually active, and not in a serious relationship, so as you can imagine, I was anxious to hear what she had to say. In this video, Prophetess Bynum explained how the very design of the woman's vagina makes her a receptacle or receiver, while the design of the man's genitals, the penis, was made to project or deposit into the receptacle. She talked about how sex is what consummates a marriage and how when we have sex with someone, we are in essence getting married to that person. If we do not end these marriages once the relationship ends, then that marriage still exists and we are not really single and ready for our next relationship. I remember sitting there with my mouth wide open after the video ended, being unable to speak for a while as my friends began discussing what we had just seen and heard. Having been raised in the Christian faith, I had heard of fornication, and I knew that I was not supposed to have sex outside of marriage, but I had never heard the message taught like that before!!! I never realized the risks I was taking and the damage I was doing to myself; not only to my physical body, but also to my emotional, mental, and spiritual body. It wasn't that I did not believe in marriage. In fact, I had planned to marry my high school boyfriend, and my parents had been married for seventeen years before my father's death. While I was greatly impacted by the video and its message, my internal needs for love and acceptance were so great that I eventually tucked it away in the recesses of my mind and continued my journey of looking for love and settling for sex. It would be many years later when I would really begin to grasp the message of that video in its entirety. As my relationship with God and myself deepened, I began to fully understand the ramifications of both casual sex and sex outside of marriage. From unwanted pregnancies and sexually transmitted diseases to the creation of unhealthy soul ties, both can have a significant life-changing impact on a woman physically, emotionally, psychologically, and spiritually.

Several years ago, one of my closest friends who I had watched the No More Sheets video with back in the early 1990s, shared an experience with me involving a guy she had dated. This friend had always been employed, had always had good credit, paid her bills on time, and had even bought her own home. Once she began dating this particular guy and having intercourse with him, she soon found that her life was beginning to mirror his life. She started having financial challenges just like him and even lost her car just like him! I was astonished because I had never heard of her having these kinds of issues before. When that relationship ended, my friend's financial situation drastically improved and quickly returned to its former state. When we began to discuss it, she explained to me that this was the result of the soul tie she had created with him. Having remembered Prophetess Bynum's No More Sheets message from all those years ago, I asked her for more information and she shared with me in detail the concept of soul ties. Fascinated, I began reading about this subject so I could know more. I discovered that soul ties are formed in various ways, but the most common is through sexual intercourse. Soul ties can be healthy as in a marriage or close friendship, or they can be unhealthy as with those that are created through fornication and adultery. I now believe that many women are struggling to overcome the effects of soul ties and are completely unaware of it. If you have ever had flashbacks of someone from your past during intercourse with a current partner or you have found yourself constantly comparing a current partner to a past partner, there may be an existing soul tie that needs to be severed. If you have taken on characteristics or developed bad habits similar to someone you previously had sex with such as cursing, drinking, drugs, overspending, lying, etc., there is most likely a soul tie. Soul ties can even transfer mental and emotional challenges from one person to another such as mood swings, depression, anger, and anxiety. As for me, I truly believe that I developed moderate to severe anxiety as the result of a soul tie with a past boyfriend who was highly anxious most of the time. Within months of us dating, I began to have anxiety attacks that would come out of nowhere. I tried everything to get rid of them until I finally realized that this was most likely the root. I then began to pray and ask God to help me break this tie and sever any attachments. Now that I am happily married to my husband who is one of the calmest, most relaxed people I know, my anxiety and fear have decreased significantly and I no longer have those attacks.

Soul ties can also be formed through covenants, vows, and agreements. The Bible refers to soul ties as "two souls being knit together." When you are married, this serves to form a closer bond between you and your spouse. If you are unmarried, you are still being "knit together" with men you may not even like, trust or want to remain connected to. If you desire to know more about soul ties, spiritual marriages, and ways to sever them, I encourage you to watch Prophetess Juanita Bynum's "No More Sheets" which is now on YouTube. There are also several great books and teachings on the subject available through Amazon and on the internet. In the workbook that will be released following this book, I will provide information on practical and spiritual techniques that will help you identify and sever any unhealthy soul ties and attachments.

Now that we have looked at the spiritual implications of sex, especially casual sex, let us also look at the physical, emotional, and mental aspects of it. Remember that physically, the design of a woman's vagina is like that of a receptacle or receiver. Even the woman's womb where babies are formed and stored was designed to carry. Not only do we as women carry our own feelings, emotions, memories, and wounds, we also tend to carry and assume responsibility for other people including our children, our spouses, our aging parents, siblings, and even friends. By this, I mean we sometimes assume and accept responsibility for their lives, their decisions, their shortcomings, and their failures. Think of the average woman and the many roles she plays, each role having its own distinct type and amount of responsibility. More so, Black women tend to carry even more responsibility than our counterparts. How many of us brag about the "S" on our chests, which is meant to imply that we are Superwomen? I used to say it myself until I began to realize that superwoman is a comic book character, a false concept, and an impossible ideal to live up to and maintain. Superwoman is also one of the ways that many Black women use to excuse and explain our lack of support and to cover up the fact that we have not yet learned to ask for what we need for fear that we won't receive it, but I will speak more about superwoman in a later chapter. For now, let's continue to examine how the concept of women as carriers and receivers from a physical perspective affects us physically, mentally, and emotionally.

When women have babies, our bodies secrete a hormone called oxytocin, better known as the bonding hormone. This bonding hormone is nature's way of helping mothers bond with their new babies. This same hormone is also secreted during sexual intercourse, thereby "bonding" a woman to her sexual partner regardless of how long she has known him, irrespective of whether there is a commitment or not, and regardless of whether this is a healthy or unhealthy relationship. Once this bonding hormone is released, women become attached to their mates willingly and unwillingly. While a woman may think it is love at first sight or something special or cosmic, it may just be her physiology doing what it does naturally. Often, I have heard women profess to be in love in the first one or two weeks of a relationship without even knowing the person with whom they were involved. I too have had that overwhelming feeling that sometimes occurs when you meet someone and there seems to be an instant attraction, when all the pieces seem to fall into place and you can't imagine anything ever going wrong... until it does. Remember, true intimacy is developed over time and it comes from experience, knowledge, and trust. So is it really love or is it just great sex?

Once a bond has been created, women may find it extremely difficult to move on if the relationship ends or becomes unhealthy or abusive. This is why it is so easy to overlook early warning signs because once sex has occurred and the bonding process has begun, insecure attachments are already forming. Think about it. If you have ever gone out with someone that you did not have sex with and the relationship ends or starts to become unhealthy, most of the time you were able to easily move on despite how wonderful it may have once seemed. Now think of a time when you have had intercourse with a man and things did not work out. Did you find yourself feeling hurt or wishing he would call? Even if things only lasted a few days, weeks or months, you may find it difficult to let go and move on and it is most likely because the bonding hormone has already created an attachment.

Steve Harvey, who is one of my favorite comedians, gameshow hosts, and motivational speakers wrote the bestselling book, *Think Like a Man, Act Like a Lady*, which was also turned into a successful movie. In the book, Steve talks about women waiting 90 days before having sex with a man, and he even compares it with the 90-day probation period companies impose on new employees. Actually, I first heard the concept of the 90-day rule on the popular TV show Girlfriends. Joan Clayton, my favorite character, had a 90-day rule, which meant she refrained from sex during the first 90 days of a relationship. This 90-day period was meant to be a time of getting to know someone before engaging in sexual intercourse or making any other serious commitments.

While Joan's relationships rarely lasted 90 days, the concept was actually a great idea. From a psychological perspective, everyone tends to present their best selves at the beginning of a relationship, the same as with a new job. However, within 60-90 days, it becomes harder for a person to hide their true selves and they will often begin to show their true colors. The internet has made this even easier and much more common because it really allows for anonymity and promoting oneself as something and someone you are not. The show Catfish is about people who pretend to be someone or something until they are "caught" and have to confess to the person who was "catfished." I often advise my girlfriends and the women I work with to adopt and implement a 90-day rule if they have decided not to wait until marriage to have sex. I would further advise anyone wanting to engage in healthier relationships to adopt your own 90-day rule because within that 90-day period, you are very likely to see that person in many different aspects. You will see how the person handles disappointment, conflict, rejection, adversity, and life in all of its many variations. While you certainly won't learn everything you need to know in 90 days, there is a good indication that you will be able to see some of the person's major personality traits and characteristics. For example, if your partner experiences a setback at work or in his finances, does he become angry and blame you, call you out of your name, or punch a hole in the wall? These are some of the warning signs and red flags many women make excuses for or overlook. Is he a workaholic? Does he only text you, but not call? Does he tend to get missing at times with little or no explanation? If he has children, how

50

does he treat them? Does he blame his ex for the relationship ending and is he always the victim? Does he respect women? Does he have a good relationship with his sister and/or mother? These are just a few things to look for and be aware of in the 90-day dating or probationary period.

Another important thing to consider in deciding to have intercourse with someone is whether the person may have a sexually transmitted disease. Even the use of condoms, while better than nothing, is still not foolproof. Oftentimes, women will get involved with someone and then after they have dated for a while will take the next step to have unprotected sex without knowing their partner's HIV or STD status or they may start off using condoms and then decide to stop using them after a while because they feel they now know and trust the person, still without knowing their partner's status. The reality is that someone's HIV status is not likely to change, so if you have unprotected sex whether in the first week or after six months, their status will likely be the same which means you have put yourself at risk for contracting it as well. I advise anyone who is sexually active to have an adult conversation with their partners about their HIV and STD status *before* engaging in sexual activity. You may even agree to be tested together so that both of you can feel comfortable knowing each other's status and have peace of mind. Again, while nothing but abstinence is 100% preventative, this is better than the alternative.

Of course, we now know that women are much more likely to contract HIV and other STDs than men who can be carriers of the disease without ever developing it themselves due in part to the makeup of our genitals. Women are receivers. Men are depositors. In addition to the risk of disease, there is also the risk of an unwanted pregnancy. I don't simply mean unwanted as in bad timing; I mean having a child with someone without intending to, like in the instance of a one night stand or becoming pregnant by someone you barely know or with whom you only have a casual relationship. Not to mention having children with men who have no interest in being fathers and may end up abandoning and rejecting the child, men who refuse to pay child support, men who may be physically or sexually abusive, or men who may have substance abuse problems, etc. We have talked about how sex can negatively affect us as women, but having children with certain partners can have lifelong effects as well. Many things are genetically passed down from parents to children, including physical illnesses and diseases, mental illnesses, substance abuse issues, and other unhealthy habits, behaviors, personality traits and characteristics. I am not implying that most men are bad fathers nor are they the sole cause of an unwanted pregnancy. At a certain age, we all know where babies come from, and both partners share equal responsibility for ensuring they avoid an unwanted pregnancy.

So you can see how rushing into sex on the first night, first week or first month may cause you to overlook things that can be life altering. Adopting a 90-day rule or choosing to wait until marriage to have sex may not be the popular thing to do, but it may be the smart thing to do. Not only will you have the opportunity to get to know your potential partner, you also get to decide whether it is worth your time and effort or if he is what you really want. You won't be confused and distracted by fleeting emotions, butterflies in the stomach or mind blowing sex. Instead, you will be able to make rational, well thought out decisions based on your head and your heart, not your genitals. Plus, you will be able to build and develop true intimacy, trust, and lasting friendship.

Courting

Growing up, my mother used to talk to my sisters and I all the time about courting and the ways in which boys and men had "courted" her in her youth. One of my mother's courting rules for us was that our "dates" were forbidden from pulling up to the house and blowing the horn for us to come out. Anyone coming to pick us up was required to get out of the car and come to the door and ring the bell. I used to think this was such a ridiculous rule and would remind my mother that courting was such an outdated concept. I never knew that my mother was doing her best to instill pride in my sisters and I and to teach us to know our worth and value. She was also teaching us to set standards and expectations of how we wanted to be treated. I can recall her advising us not to live with men without being married. "Why buy the cow if you can get the milk for free?" was one of her favorite sayings. As much as I rebelled against her teachings growing up, these are now some of the very concepts of which I strongly believe in and advocate.

Some of her lessons I learned naturally and others came as the result of much trial and error, mostly error. For instance, I tried living with two guys only to have both end miserably. I also started allowing men to blow the horn in the driveway and not get out and ring the doorbell. I began "meeting" men out for dinner or drinks instead of having them come pick me up. I know we are living in different times now and you may not want everyone knowing where you live initially, but I also know that men enjoy the chase and were designed to pursue a woman, so when you agree to "meet" him out instead of insisting that he picks you up, you are compromising yourself and shortening the chase.

I constantly compromised my integrity and my virtue and ended up broken-hearted time and again. Over time, I began to understand that my mother hadn't been all wrong and that courting had some merit to it. So when I met my husband, I decided to do things a bit differently. I did not allow my body or my emotions or the butterflies in my stomach to lead me and guide my decisions. I adopted my own 90-day rule (actually it was closer to 120 days) and what I learned about life, men, and myself during that time was absolutely life changing, and I have never been the same, nor do I view relationships the same.

In this chapter, we have looked at many different aspects of sex and intimacy. We have defined and explored both in detail including the emotional, physical, and mental aspects; we have also learned about spiritual implications and the concept of soul ties and spiritual marriages, and we have even learned ways to honor and protect ourselves by waiting and taking the time to really get to know someone. I always remind women that if a man is really the right one, he will still be the right one 90 days later or even six months or a year later. Don't be swayed by your fears of missing out or fear that he will move on. The right man will realize that you are worth it and will stay around to see where things go. So give yourself the time to get to know him so that you can truly decide for yourself if it is worth it to risk your heart and possibly your life.

Chapter 4

Superwoman

Many women, especially Black women, have fallen in love with the term "superwoman". A term meant to imply that we have powers that are somehow above ordinary issues and conditions. In this chapter, I will define superwoman, her strengths and her weaknesses, and discuss how this can interfere with her ability to attract and maintain healthy, supportive, and loving relationships with others and with herself.

Superwoman is the single mom who takes care of herself and her children with or without the support of the father. Superwoman is the wife who takes on the responsibilities of everyone in her household including her spouse and her children. She also takes on responsibilities outside the house by caring for elderly parents, neighbors, church members, siblings, friends, and anyone else she feels depends on her for their own happiness, support, and fulfillment. Superwoman is the woman who has overcome tragedy, trauma, abuse, discrimination, poverty, low self-esteem, and now feels she has a responsibility to the world, so she readily accepts the mission and calling to save those who are still lost and seeking. Superwoman is the woman who constantly takes on new projects, overworks herself, over commits, over schedules, and over compensates. Superwoman proudly references the "S" on her chest and her ability to keep going in the face of adversity to "do what she has to do." She is quick to jump in and assist where needed, quick to place others ahead of herself and quick to give tirelessly even at the expense of her own physical, mental, and emotional health, happiness, and well-being.

As I mentioned previously, my mother was a superwoman, fiercely independent and easily the strongest woman I have ever known. A single mother of seven children and my oldest nephew, I often remember her doing what she had to do, making a way out of no way and continuing on in spite of financial struggles, parenting challenges, work-related stress, and even health problems. I vividly recall her managing our household on a shoestring budget with the income she earned working part time and then full time with the school district as a housekeeper. We didn't have the finest things in life, and it seemed like there were always repairs needed in the house or with the car, but we never went without the necessities. Looking back on it and knowing what she earned, I am amazed at how she was able to make ends meet with so little, but she did. Even when she became ill with pneumonia and later developed COPD which required her to wear oxygen daily, my mother the superwoman persevered. She continued to drive everywhere she needed to go, continued to wash clothes and clean the house, and kept preparing Sunday and holiday meals for her children, grandchildren, and anyone else who stopped by for a plate of food. My mother was superwoman to our family and me, and that was what was modeled for me day in and day out. That was what I understood a woman to be. What I didn't see was how tired she had to have been some days, how weary and worn down, how hopeless or helpless she may have felt at times, and how she must have longed for some additional support, a vacation, or just a day off to lay it all down if only for 24 hours. My mother, like many superwomen I know, was great at showcasing her superpowers to her family, friends, colleagues, and the world. However, she was not good at accepting and displaying that it is perfectly okay sometimes to lay it all down, take a day off, do for yourself and allow yourself to be cared for and supported. Perhaps she was afraid. Perhaps most superwomen are afraid. Afraid that no one will be there for them; afraid that no one can do it the way they would; afraid that it will make them appear vulnerable, incompetent or weak; afraid that their families, children, jobs, and communities will fall apart if they are not there holding everything in place. However, being afraid does not make superwomen invincible or immune to basic human emotions and conditions such as illness, despair, depression, sadness, anger, frustration, helplessness, and hopelessness. It does not make her super-human, nor is she above needing support and time to herself. I understand that for some women, time off may be a luxury they cannot afford because their time off is usually spent with sick children, spouses, siblings, or parents. When she is not feeling well, superwoman pushes through and goes to work anyway. She gets up every morning, makes breakfast, lunches, signs papers, makes coffee, irons clothes, and maybe even does her children's hair. She ignores the aches and pains in her own body and the weariness in her soul as she prepares for yet another day of doing for others and not herself.

There is a cost to being a superhero, a price to be paid. While we marvel at comic book characters and even real life superwomen, what we don't always see is the toll this role is taking on their bodies, their minds, and emotions, not to mention their relationships and families. Superwoman may become increasingly anxious, depressed, stressed, overwhelmed, irritable, bitter, and resentful as she continuously denies her own happiness and fulfillment. She becomes so good at playing the role that others expect her to play that she cannot and will not risk people knowing that behind her tough exterior and seemingly infallible façade is a woman longing for time off, a moment to herself, or an opportunity to cry, scream or yell. Superwoman has not yet learned to give herself permission to be flawed, to be human, and to be imperfect as she hides her fears, her insecurities, her doubts, and her stuff in her efforts to focus on "doing" instead of simply "being."

A few months ago, I saw a young woman wearing a shirt that said, "A bad hair day kind of girl," and I remember thinking, "wow, how great is that to give yourself permission to be off, to be imperfect, and to have a bad hair day." To be what Tyra Banks calls flaw-some (knowing your flaws and accepting that you are awesome anyway). In my private practice, I often work with women who are struggling with perfectionism and have at some point in life adopted the belief that they are somehow inadequate, lacking, not good enough, wrong, damaged and broken. As a result, they believe they have to be perfect in order to overcompensate for their shortcomings. This often causes them to be controlling, bossy, possessive, and demanding and they are always striving for perfection within themselves and expecting it from those around them. These women are rarely off and are constantly in "doing" mode and rarely in "being" mode. Difficult to please, they may end up ruining their relationships because as they strive to be perfect, they also demand perfection in their relationships which causes the men in their lives to feel as if they can never do enough or be enough.

While all superwomen do not struggle with perfectionism, a majority of them do, which is why they cannot give themselves permission to be vulnerable and ask for help. While being great at giving of their time, resources, talents and attention, they are often terrible at receiving as their sense of worth and value is often fused with their need to be needed. They may even feel guilty and undeserving when someone attempts to give and do for them. They can also become discouraged and resentful as they reflect on how much they do for others and rarely receive in return. Superwomen are often unwilling and unable to receive compliments, acknowledgment, support and assistance, and may even reject it. Then there are the superwomen who derive their sense of worth and value from the external validation and acknowledgment they receive from the roles they play in other people's lives. Sadly, if the role changes or ends, they are left feeling empty, unappreciated, angry, and often resentful. Superwoman can be so busy taking care of others that she neglects herself. She either doesn't have time for a relationship or she attracts partners who are needy and dependent.

As we bring this chapter to a close on superwoman, know that not all aspects of being a superwoman are negative, bad or self-defeating. One of the things I admire most about us as Black women is our strength, resilience, and our fortitude as well as our dedication to our families and our mates. We really are made up of some good stuff even if society would have us think differently. My hope is that if you are a superwoman, you learn that there are healthier ways of doing and being in the world and that you are not always required to sacrifice yourself in the service of others. You can learn to balance your life, say no, set boundaries and make time for yourself. Make self-care a priority and a necessity. Get pedicures, massages, practice yoga, meditation, deep breathing, and other relaxation techniques on a regular and consistent basis without explanation, justification, or apology. As you learn to give yourself permission to be vulnerable, nurtured, cared for and supported, you can learn to develop healthy, loving, and mutually beneficial relationships.

Chapter 5

Miss Independent

I still remember the first time I heard Independent by Beyoncé and Miss Independent by Ne-Yo. I danced, chanted, sang along, and pumped my fist to music that encouraged women to be independent and have their own. Many women today are proudly celebrating being a boss, running their businesses, making a lot of money, and standing on their own two feet. Having been raised by a single mother, I grew up being taught to stand on my own two feet, so when these songs came out, I was excited to proclaim my independence along with everyone else. But then I remembered all the times I had been criticized for being "too independent." I can still recall some of my past romantic partners complaining that I didn't know how to submit and didn't know how to let a man be a man. I remember feeling like I could do everything a man could do and so at the end of the day, I really didn't need one. After all, my mother had been single for much of my life and even when she had dated, she continued to work, take care of us, and "have her own." She didn't rely on men in that way which was sort of ironic because she always told stories of how my father never wanted her to work. She would jokingly tell us that she only went to work to buy things for herself that he refused to buy for her. So here I was, this woman who grew up without a father or a   father figure being taught by a strong, independent, single mother to always stand on my own two feet and yet somehow I was supposed to know when to be submissive and let a man be a man. Needless to say, I made a lot of mistakes. There were power struggles in many of my relationships. My male friends were telling me that I was dating insecure men because a secure man would not be intimidated or threatened by a strong, independent woman. I wasn't sure what to think or what to do. Half the time I blamed the men and the other half of the time, I blamed myself. The truth was, I didn't understand submission or what it meant to let a man be a man. I didn't even like the way the word *submission* sounded because I took it as having to bow down to a man which was a bit too reminiscent of slavery for me. Besides, I had grown up with four brothers, and lots of male cousins and the girls were always competing with the boys. At one point in time, I could outrun and out wrestle the boys in my family who were close to me in age, and I was smarter than the majority of them in school, so I could not imagine a situation where it made sense to me to submit and give them the upper hand. Besides the fact that I had been sexually abused and raped by men, had a string of broken relationships in my past, and had unresolved issues of rejection and abandonment from my father and stepfather, I didn't even trust men or like them all that much. How was I supposed to allow one to lead me? Actually, I viewed men as the enemy. I had this me against them or rather them against me mentality, and I was not going to let them win or dominate me. However, deep down I was really longing to have someone cover me, protect me, understand me, and allow me to be my strong, untamed, independent self without feeling threatened and intimidated. Because I was broken and had no real male role models, I attracted a lot of men who were broken themselves. Some of them had also grown up without fathers and had never been taught how to really love and respect a woman. Or they had fathers who were physically, verbally, and emotionally abusive or neglectful to women. Others grew up with strong, independent mothers like mine who had done their best to raise them the correct way, but as we now know, it is very hard for a woman to raise a man. I saw this with my own mother who did her best to raise my brothers the right way, and yet I frequently observed them disrespecting women and being verbally and even physically abusive. My brothers, like some of the men I dated, had their own insecurities and were trying to discover ways to become men without male guidance as I was learning how to become a woman without it. Looking back on it and knowing what I now know, I believe we were all longing for the same things in life, which was to feel loved, wanted, accepted, validated, and affirmed. Remember when I talked about the roles fathers play in our lives as children? Not only is it about what they provide for us, it is also about the examples they set for us to follow. If a girl grows up having a father care for and provide for her while leading the family, then she will instinctively understand how to allow a man to lead, guide, and provide for her. Likewise, if a male grows up watching his father provide those things for the family, he will instinctively grow up understanding his position and how he is expected to treat the women in his life. He is likely not to be insecure or intimidated by a strong woman, nor will he have a need to prove his position or his power because when you own your power, there is no need to fight for it. My husband is a great example of this. I recall a time not long ago when he was chosen to coach our son's baseball team. He was one of the youngest fathers out there and at the first practice, some of the older fathers sort of jumped in and took the lead before he arrived at practice. My husband didn't walk in feeling threatened or defensive nor did he argue or even remind them that he was the head coach. He simply walked out on the field, assumed his rightful position, and commanded their respect.

As you may have figured out by now, Miss Independent and Superwoman have a lot of things in common, but in order to understand Miss Independent in more detail, let us look at the different types of independent women I have met and come to know. The most obvious may be the well-educated, high performing professional woman who has earned her position of power and leadership both personally and professionally. This woman owns her own home, drives a luxury car, and makes executive decisions on a daily basis. She is a Boss. Then there is the independent woman who never had anyone to depend on and learned that she could only depend on herself. She may be playing the role of mother and father to her children and the role of man and woman in society. She cooks, cleans, and cares for the household while also having to manage the finances, discipline the children, check homework, repair broken appliances, and even argue with the mechanic when the car breaks down. Next, we have the independent woman who plays the role of being independent, but really has never discovered her value and so she tells herself she doesn't need a man, and therefore doesn't even expect or require the men in her life to be men. She may have trust issues, self-esteem issues, control issues, and most likely daddy issues. This woman often feels that she has something to prove and will either remain single or hook up with a dependent man to prove her strength and independence. Lastly, there are the independent women who may date a man for twenty plus years and may even live with him, but will never marry for fear of giving up her independence. As a result, she has no real rights, privileges or security even if when the man dies. Sadly, I recently saw this play out when my brother passed away. He had been living with his girlfriend for the past fourteen years, but because they never married or put anything on paper, she ended up feeling hurt and frustrated when she realized she had very little power when it came to planning his final arrangements. I also had a client once who had been dating a man who was still legally married to his wife. She had been with this man for over twenty years, but had never made any legal arrangements or pushed him to divorce his wife and marry her. When this man died, his wife would not even allow her to sit with the family at the funeral or assist in any of the preparations. Despite the years she had invested in this relationship, because the law only recognizes the legal spouse, she was forced to mourn him from a distance.

In my personal and professional experience, I have met and known the women with advanced degrees, six-figure salaries, and high-powered positions in the workplace to the round the way girls with something to prove and the baby mamas having babies by men who may or may not provide for them. Some of them are married, while others are still single, and although they may differ in some aspects, many of their struggles are the same. While the single independent woman is struggling to figure out why she cannot seem to maintain a healthy relationship and/or get married, the married independent woman is having constant power struggles with her husband. The single independent woman is often criticized for being too strong, too independent, too bossy, too controlling, and lacking the ability or willingness to submit and let a man be a man, while the married woman is often criticized for the same character traits. These women, like myself, are sometimes caught between standing on their own two feet and either remaining single for the rest of their lives or constantly arguing and battling with their husbands for position and power. I have lived their dilemmas and have seen it play out in the worst ways in my own life having been taught by my own mother to be independent and not depend on a man to be, do, and have. I have been told that I was too strong, too independent, too outspoken, too controlling, too "smart," too this, and too that, all of which really did a number on my already crippled self-esteem. I often found myself wondering what I was doing wrong and how I could change myself to be this woman that men seemed to want without completely compromising myself. The truth is that I was strong, independent, smart, outspoken and used to being in control. I had grown up as the middle child in a family of seven constantly fighting for position. I learned early on how to stand on my own. How was I supposed to unlearn those things or abandon who I was for a man? I asked this question and others in my quest for love and happiness, and God and the universe answered. I wasn't ready for the answers I received, but being open and vulnerable to these life lessons changed my perspectives on life, on marriage, on submission, on men, and on myself. One of the biggest lessons I learned is that my guy friends had been right. A secure man is not threatened by a strong, independent woman, but a woman does need to let a man be a man unless she desires to continue to be the man in her life. I love to tell the groups of women I speak to that while I am grateful to know how to change a tire, check the oil in a car, cut the grass, and pay the bills, the truth is I don't want to, and I praise God I no longer have to. When my husband is outside in the heat of summer cutting grass and taking care of the lawn, I am inside our air conditioned house sitting on the sofa watching TV. When there is an issue with the car, I no longer panic or give it a second thought. Once I mention it, my husband will tell me to drive one of the other cars for a few days until my car is repaired and returned. My husband covers our family and he provides us with safety, stability, and structure. This is what I have come to learn about submission. It is not allowing a man to control you, dominate you, abuse you or make you into a doormat. It is not acting as if you are ignorant, inadequate or helpless so that he can feel strong. To me, submission is an act of trust. My husband was not and is not threatened by me and has never tried to dominate or intimidate me which made it easy to submit to him. I didn't submit out of fear or weakness, I submitted out of love, trust, and respect. If you are an independent woman and you are afraid to submit for fear that you will have to give up your independence, your position, and your power, please understand that submission is not an act of attrition or a sign of weakness. It is an act of will, courage, trust and respect.

In conclusion, I am not advocating that any woman should completely give up her independence and become solely dependent on a man. I feel we all should be able to stand on our own if ever necessary, but I also want independent women to accept and understand that men are not the enemy and we do not have to be in competition or power struggles with them. Black love still exists, and Black men and women can have respectful, loving, supportive, and healthy relationships with one another.

Chapter 6

The Angry Black Woman

Many of us are familiar with the stereotype of the angry Black woman. As I write this chapter, Iyanla Vanzant is addressing this issue on her popular television show, "Iyanla: Fix My Life." While I have not watched this particular series (as I like to write from a place of originality and authenticity), I am sure that she is touching on many of the same topics I will highlight in this section.

I don't remember ever hearing about the angry Black woman until I was older in life. I am also not sure if the guys I dated ever considered me to be an angry Black woman. If they did, it was never one of the many complaints that were shared with me. While they may not have stated it, the truth of the matter is that I was angry inside and I am certain from time to time, this anger showed up in my relationships. However, I was so eager to please, that I am sure I probably found ways to mask my anger with other more acceptable emotions. Even if I was unaware of it myself and even if the men I dated chose not to mention it, the truth is that I was an angry Black woman. I was angry that I grew up without a father and was never validated, approved of or affirmed throughout most of my childhood. I was angry that I wasn't my mother's favorite child and that my mother was never able to express her emotions or tell me she loved me. While she certainly demonstrated her love for me by always being present at my activities and events, I sometimes longed and needed to hear the words as well. I was angry that I grew up in a predominantly white town where I wasn't expected to excel academically. A town where one of my white male classmates, whose parents were both doctors, was amazed and upset when I outperformed him in school which sent me a silent message that I should "under-perform." I was angry that I wasn't making the money I thought I would make after going to college and graduate school and that my life wasn't working out the way I planned. I was angry that men just did not seem to "get" me and I never felt the freedom to just be myself. I was angry that I had been raped in college and sexually abused as a child and that my mother never knew and my perpetrators continued on in life as if nothing had occurred.

I was carrying and harboring a lot of anger, bitterness, and resentment and I witnessed a lot of anger in the women around me as well. It wasn't until I began my work as a therapist and life coach that I began to understand that underneath anger usually lies a host of other emotions such as hurt, sadness, disappointment, betrayal, fear, injustice, abandonment, rejection, and inadequacy and that if you can get to those emotions and heal them, the anger will begin to resolve itself. I have also learned that anger is a more acceptable emotion than sadness or fear because it gives us a false sense of power and control and the other emotions tend to make us feel helpless and vulnerable.

I knew the reasons behind my own personal anger, but I wondered, why were the women around me and many other Black women in society so angry? Why did their faces have a perpetual scowl on them and why was their demeanor sometimes so aggressive and abrasive? Furthermore, what was this anger doing to their relationships, their children and their lives?

Having always had a love of history, I decided to explore the history and evolution of the Black woman in America so that I could gain a better understanding of who we were and who we have become. I wanted to shed some light on this because once again I found me and my sistas getting a bad rap without the benefit of an explanation or understanding. Let me first point out that I believe there are many angry Black men as well, but since anger seems to be a more acceptable emotion in men than it is in women in our society, I intend to only focus on the angry Black woman or the ABW.

Let us begin with the African slave trade which according to Wikipedia, began in the 15th century and lasted through the 19th century. The Portuguese were the first to engage in the slave trade when they completed the first slave voyage from Africa to the Americas in 1526, but the British, the French, the Spanish, and the Dutch also engaged in purchasing slaves from West Africa that were shipped and sold as cargo. Some estimate that at least 12 million slaves were shipped across the Atlantic although others believe the number to be closer to 20 million. Upon arrival, slaves were then subject to being separated from their spouses, children, friends, neighbors, and other loved ones and sold to slave owners who stripped them of their dignity, culture, language, religion, and identity. Slaves endured harsh verbal, physical, and emotional treatment, brutal work conditions and poor living conditions in addition to being denied the right to vote, the right to read and get an education, and even the right to legally marry. In situations where marriage was permitted, the marriages were not considered legal, and the possibility always existed for one of them to be sold away never to see each other or their children again. I believe this ever-present reality severely impacted the Black family unit as well as began the decline of marriages and relationships between Black women and men. Fast forward to the end of slavery and reconstruction when you had many Black men leaving their wives and children behind in search of employment and land forcing Black women to become the matriarchs of their families. These matriarchal homes continued on during the civil rights movement and still exist today. As previously mentioned, 72% of African-American children reside in single parent homes in the Black community. Couple that with the mass incarceration of Black men, high unemployment rates, and the number of Black males dying from disease, interpersonal violence, alcoholism and drug abuse, and you can begin to see the impact on our families and relationships in general.

I believe that because so many Black women were forced to depend on themselves and some may have even decided they didn't really need men; relationships became a constant power struggle between Black men and women. The sad truth is that none of us ever asked for this. Black women didn't ask to become the heads of our households or to be single parents raising our sons and daughters. We didn't ask to have to be so strong, invincible, independent, or even "super" women. We didn't ask to carry burdens of guilt, shame, mistrust, betrayal, bitterness, and resentment from our pasts. However, we did learn to adapt to our circumstances and to draw upon our inner resources of strength and resilience in order to survive. Instead of embracing the fear, disappointment, sadness, loneliness, hopelessness, and helplessness we may have sometimes felt and experienced, we buried those feelings behind emotional walls of protection so that we would not appear to be too vulnerable because vulnerability was seen as a sign of weakness.

I believe that the burdens Black women had to carry and the pain that we have endured along with the disappointments, high expectations, discrimination, rejection, and lack of support have all helped create the persona of the angry Black woman who is often unfairly misunderstood and poorly misaligned. I am not saying that these are excuses for being angry, exhibiting bad behavior or even as a concession and admission of truth, because the reality is that not all Black women are angry. While it is true that many of us have been disempowered and disenfranchised, we are not all angry, hard, mouthy or bitter any more than all Caucasian women are slim, attractive, passive, and submissive. There are variations among all women. Is it fair to say that some Black women are angry? Absolutely. As Kimberly Elise's character stated in Tyler Perry's movie "Diary of a Mad Black Woman," some of us are mad as hell! Perhaps a better question to ask is, "Are we mad as hell or are we just tired?" Are we tired of not being viewed as attractive by society, the beauty industry, white men and even some

Black men? Are we tired of carrying the burdens of the men we love, be it our mates, our brothers, and our sons? Are we tired of having to compete twice as hard as other women and men in the workplace only to be viewed as half as good? Are we tired of our own men treating us as if we are only good enough to date, have babies with, and play house with but not marry? Are we tired of raising children on our own while our children's fathers complain about or refuse to pay child support? Are we tired of being emulated by women of other ethnicities who adopt our style without giving us any credit for it? Are we just tired of being overlooked, under-appreciated, invisible and tolerated?

I believe that Black women have created and continue to create emotional walls to protect our inner vulnerability in order to withstand the challenges we face as a double minority in America. I also feel that some of us have surrendered our sweet spirits and rejected our femininity, because femininity for us may be a luxury we cannot afford and a privilege to which we have no rights. Over time, I believe we became so accustomed to hiding our emotions, insecurities, and weaknesses that we eventually began to disconnect from who we really are on the inside. Yes, some of us are strong, resilient, tough, sassy, loud, opinionated, and even bossy. Some are quiet, gentle, sweet, and soft-spoken while others are a wonderful mixture of various aspects of strength and femininity. We are multi-faceted, creative, unique, soulful, proud, strong, intelligent, thoughtful, prayerful, faithful, and loyal and we can and will overcome whatever life throws at us. So instead of society and even some of our own men judging and criticizing us based on the myths, stereotypes, lies, misperceptions, and what they see on the outside, perhaps it is worth getting to know who we really are on the inside. However, in order for others to come to know who we are instead of what we portray, we have to be willing to face and confront our issues and resolve whatever it is that is making us and keeping us angry. We cannot spend the rest of our lives mad at our mamas, our daddies, society, men, and ourselves. We cannot sit by idly waiting and expecting others to tear down or traverse our emotional walls, ride in on a white horse and rescue us. We cannot hope that the world will suddenly understand what we have been through and become kinder to us. The responsibility for healing is and always has been ours. Others can assist, but they cannot do the work for us. We have to accept and assume responsibility for our own healing and do the inner work to release our anger and become whole. As we work to heal ourselves, we are also able to heal and improve the relationships we have with our men, our co-workers, our family members, our friends, and our children. We cannot control other people, their actions or how they view us, but we can become better for ourselves and our children. Our sons and daughters are watching and need to see that we are not invincible, that we do have normal feelings and emotions and that we too are allowed to be vulnerable. Our daughters need to know and accept that it is okay to be strong and feminine so that they can enter in and enjoy healthy relationships of their own that are devoid of anger, bitterness, and resentment. This is how we overcome the stereotype of the angry Black woman, by healing ourselves, our daughters, and our relationships one at a time.

Chapter 7

Bag Lady

In the previous chapter we talked about the angry Black woman, and hopefully, I was able to shed some light on the underlying factors that I feel may be contributing to her anger, while also highlighting the need to move beyond anger towards healing and wholeness. In this chapter, we will more fully explore not only anger, but other emotions such as sadness, guilt, shame, blame, resentment, and even grief. I will talk about how emotions affect our moods, thoughts, and behaviors which may influence our self-esteem, self-worth, self-perception, and self-image which in turn affects how we interact, relate, and communicate in our relationships. We will discuss women with mental and emotional health challenges, women who have experienced childhood trauma such as rape and abuse, and women with mommy issues and daddy issues of abandonment, rejection, and emotional neglect.

In her 2000 debut single, Erykah Badu introduced us to the concept of "bag ladies." Erykah sings of bag ladies who are carrying so much stuff they are going to miss their bus. She continues singing about how the bags are getting in the bag lady's way, crowding her man's space, and even causing men to run away. The bridge of the song advises us to "pack light." When this song debuted, I think many of us were clueless as to what it was really about and I wasn't sure myself when I initially heard it. I liked it, and it was catchy, but even when I began to listen and understand what she was really saying, I resisted it. Erykah, in her Baduism kinda way, was describing women who are walking around with emotional and psychological baggage and carrying that baggage from relationship to relationship. I also believe that the bag lady is often inwardly hoping that someone else will carry her emotional bags with her and for her. The bag lady may not only expect this, but she may demand it as a condition of her relationship. I understand that none of us want to look at ourselves in this way, but the reality is that many of us are carrying emotional baggage that causes us to be angry, bitter, resentful, hard, tough, emotionally detached, needy, sad, and depressed. I was definitely a bag lady and some days still am, along with many of my clients, colleagues, neighbors, friends, and family. Sometimes it seems as if we are all working to overcome something. Life can be tough, and most of us were not taught how to deal with our issues and heal from the traumas, toxic emotions, and self-defeating behaviors in our lives. Many people who have experienced painful things in childhood have never had the opportunity to resolve those things. As a result, the negative impact and effects of those things just continue to grow with them and within them. I frequently work with clients in my office who are in their 40s, 50s, and 60s who are still trapped by painful childhood experiences. They are still wrestling with feelings of guilt, shame, blame, abandonment, rejection, and neglect. One of the resources I frequently recommend is Karol K. Truman's book "Feelings Buried Alive Never Die." The basic premise behind this book is that just because we have buried, hidden, stored, and ignored our childhood traumas, memories, feelings, and emotions, doesn't mean they are dead. These things have simply been buried alive and are still living just beneath the surface of our lives waiting to be awakened or triggered by an event, memory or tragedy. They can ruin our relationships because they often show up as a reaction to something current when they are really the result of something long hidden and seemingly forgotten. They show up as trust issues, control issues, jealousy, insecurities, codependency, bitterness, resentment, anger, and sadness. If left unresolved, they begin to define and determine every encounter we have with the people in our lives from our neighbors and coworkers to our friends and partners. While our conscious minds may be telling us one thing about a person or a situation, these hidden feelings are telling a whole different story, and that story normally becomes the one we believe and accept. Sometimes this can be as subtle as having trust issues with a current partner because of the infidelity of a past partner. People living with buried emotions can have an array of problems ranging from depression and anxiety to bipolar disorder and other mental and emotional health challenges. Getting to the roots of these buried feelings and trapped emotions and resolving them can have a significant impact on a person's healing and subsequently, on their relationships.

I work with a large number of women, and men, who were victims of childhood/teenage rape or abuse and these individuals often continue to struggle in their adult relationships. They are frequently plagued with issues from irrational fears of rejection and abandonment that cause them to be needy and clingy to self-rejection, self-loathing, and even self-hatred. Some people with childhood trauma grow up to struggle with moderate to severe mental and emotional challenges while others may turn to drugs and alcohol to escape their pasts and the painful emotions buried inside of them. They may be promiscuous or turn to prostitution and the sex industry because they believe themselves to be worthless. However, not all adult victims of childhood rape and abuse have such severe struggles, but many still suffer from the negative effects of their trauma. As I mentioned previously, probably forty percent of the clients I work with, male and female, have been violated in some way during their childhoods. I call them the "walking wounded." They are our sisters, mothers, grandmothers, aunts, nieces, cousins, friends, and spouses. They may even be us. From the outside, no one would ever guess because they have learned to mask the inner guilt and shame with the right clothing, hair, and make-up. They may even drive the right cars, live in the right neighborhoods, and even hold the right jobs, but inwardly, they are still wounded little girls silently crying out for help.

Until very recently, I too still struggled with the effects of my past and it took a while for me to learn and understand that my abuse was not my fault and to no longer allow it to define my relationships with men, with others, and with myself. For years, I buried the feelings associated with my abuse as I tried to convince myself that I was strong enough to handle it, that I didn't need to tell, and that I was saving my family the embarrassment. Sadly, in my shame and secrecy, I was also indirectly protecting my abusers from the punishment they rightly deserved. I was twenty-nine years old when I finally told my mother and I fully exhaled that day for the first time since I was a child as I released the enormous weight of that burden. It has taken me many more years to work through the issues from my past, and I continue my journey of growth and healing to this day. Working through my abuse has helped me understand my previous relationship challenges, and I have been able to understand my unhealthy relationship patterns and behaviors such as my tendency to date jealous, insecure, controlling men or emotionally detached and unavailable men. As I began to own and accept my issues of low self-esteem and low self-worth, I was able to clearly see how I had allowed myself to be disrespected, devalued, and mistreated. I could also see what was guiding and determining my decisions and how I was attracting the same types of guys no matter how much I kept telling myself that the next one would be different.

Emotional Challenges

I remember once hearing Oprah say that depression is a luxury some people cannot afford. I think for Black women, it is a luxury we are not "allowed" which goes back to the concept and myth of the strong Black superwoman. The reality is that Black women are human and that humanness makes us susceptible to the same psychological and emotional conditions as the rest of humanity. Because we are susceptible to the same human emotions of despair, unhappiness, anxiety, sadness, grief, guilt, loneliness, insecurity, inadequacy, anger, resentment, inferiority, and low self-esteem, we are also susceptible to suffering with mild to severe depression, bi-polar disorder, anxiety or what we like to call "bad nerves," and a host of other mental, psychological, and emotional challenges. In fact, I believe that the root of a lot of the Black woman's anger could be undiagnosed and untreated depression. Depression has sometimes been referred to as "anger turned inward" or anger against the self. Not only is the anger turned inward against the self, but self-blame, self-hatred, and self-loathing usually show up in connection to these feelings as well.

The type of depression I am referring to in this chapter is not the occasional blues nor is it the normal response to a negative event such as death, divorce or loss of employment. It is perfectly normal to feel despair or despondency in response to such incidents, but if those feelings continue to linger or worsen, then that becomes a cause for concern. If someone begins to feel suicidal or homicidal following a tragic event, they should be advised to seek help immediately. Some people also suffer from dysthymia or low-level depression that may be mild in nature, but never really goes away. People with dysthymia may continue to work, go to school, and carry on normal lives, but they live with a general feeling of discontentment.

Symptoms of depression may include, but are not limited to:

82

✓ Irritability
✓ Agitation and being easily frustrated
✓ Lack of interest in normal activities
✓ Low energy and fatigue
✓ Excessive sleep or insomnia
✓ Weight gain or weight loss
✓ Sadness and crying
✓ Restlessness and anxiety
✓ Social isolation, not wanting to be around others
✓ Thoughts of suicide or wanting to die

Unfortunately, Black women usually do not like to admit to having depression or any other mental illness and are less likely to seek treatment. It goes back to my belief that Black women may feel they are not "allowed" to be depressed. Admitting to depression and seeking treatment for it is seen as a sign of weakness in the Black community and other minority communities. Some people may even struggle with their spiritual views as it relates to depression and mental illness. They may feel or be told that depression is something they just need to pray about and keep to themselves. While I am huge believer and advocate of prayer for my clients and myself, I encourage them to pray as they continue to seek treatment, and not as a replacement to seeking treatment. In the same way that someone would follow the advice of their doctor if they were given a diagnosis of cancer or diabetes, seeking treatment for a psychological or emotional issue is no different. It is not an admission of weakness. I tell clients all the time that it takes a huge amount of courage to come into my office and share their ugliest, darkest, and dirtiest secrets. There is no amount of weakness in that. I have found that those who take that first step and continue to come and engage in treatment also become the ones who normally walk out of my office months or maybe even a year later with a whole new perspective on life. In fact, I see it as one of the highest forms of self-love and self-care a person can give herself or himself. The truth is that prayer and mental health treatment can work wonders together in helping someone improve mentally and emotionally just as chemotherapy and insulin can work wonders for people in improving their physical health. We live in a physical world inside of physical bodies, and these bodies have brains in them that sometimes get out of balance, which can affect our thoughts, moods, feelings, and behaviors. When you add to that poor diets, environmental pollutants, and the daily stresses of work and life, then it is no wonder that we sometimes may be in need of extra support. Do not stop praying and seeking God in regards to your depression, anxiety or any other mental or emotional health issue, but also do not discredit the amazing work of psychiatrists, psychologists, social workers, and professional counselors like myself who are passionate about what we do and the people we serve. While I cannot promise that everyone's experience with therapy or medication will be positive, I encourage you to keep searching if the need is there. Don't stop because of one bad experience just as you wouldn't stop eating if you had a bad meal or received poor service at a restaurant. I do not know of one client in my experience who has regretted getting rid of their junk and getting their lives back. Not one. In fact, the only regret most of them have is not having done something sooner.

Perhaps the whole premise behind this chapter on bag ladies is that we as women must be willing to deal with and overcome our own stuff before we can successfully and fully engage in healthy relationships. While there are exceptions to every rule and some women have been blessed to meet and marry partners who have loved them through their mess, there are many more women who have yet to meet their Boaz.

As I mentioned in a previous chapter, when you are one of the walking wounded or you are struggling with a mental or emotional issue, you will enter into relationships with others expecting and seeking them to fulfill you, complete you, and rescue you. The problem with this is that usually the other person has no idea how to fulfill you or may even resent the expectation that they must fulfill you. The other problem with this is that when someone else does your work for you, then you are always dependent on them to continue to do your work and you never get the benefit of doing it yourself. Let me assure you, there are many benefits to doing your work and filling your own cup! If you are feeling empty or half full, you will often seek friends, family, romantic partners, and other people to fill your cup. You may also strive to fill your cup with personal and professional accomplishments, material items or even food, sex, alcohol or drugs. The problem with this is that even if those people or those things cause you to feel full, it is usually only temporary. You then either have to constantly go back to them for continued reassurance and fulfillment or seek it from other external sources if those are unavailable. You may also become angry and feel slighted or unsupported by those people. In truth, it is never anyone else's job to fulfill us or sustain us. The people in our lives should add to our lives, not become the source of our happiness and our existence because if those people should ever leave us either voluntarily or involuntarily, then we will go right back to having that half empty cup. Or if those people simply cannot and do not fill us up, we will invariably end up right back where we started. If you do the work and fill your own cup from the inside out, you never have to worry about needing someone to stay in your life or remain a certain way in order for you to be happy and fulfilled. Now, when you enter into relationships with others, you will already have a full cup. If those people do not add to your cup or begin to take away from it, it may still hurt, but it won't destroy you. And because you have learned to replenish it yourself from the inside out, you always know how to refill it and you never have to fear being thirsty again. None of this is meant to imply that we do not need other people. We were created to be in relationship with one another, especially women, but the people in our lives are there to enrich us, help us grow and to make this journey called life even sweeter. However, if you find yourself constantly feeling defeated, depleted, emotionally exhausted, wounded, and empty in your relationships, you must be willing to do a self-assessment in order to determine if the relationship is worth staying in and fighting for.

The first thing I would advise you to consider is, "Am I asking and expecting something from this person that I am not willing to offer and provide for myself?"

Sometimes people enter into relationships feeling worthless and devalued and get angry if their mates fail to fix this and make them feel valued. While none of us should ever choose to be de-valued in a relationship, a lot of times people treat you the way you treat yourself. In other words, it is not a man's job, or anyone else's to make you feel valued if you do not value yourself. It is not his job to make you feel respected if you are not willing to respect yourself. It is not his job to build your self-esteem, rid you of your jealousy and insecurities, or make up for what you did not receive from your parents. I shared my own story of emotional lack, and I know that I am not alone. Many of us have experienced emotional deficits or longed for things we needed and never received. When I work with couples, I often help them identify their love language because many of the conflicts in relationships can be eliminated if people learn to communicate more effectively and understanding and speaking each other's love language can greatly assist in that. For example, if a woman's love language is Words of Affirmation and she grew up never receiving words of affirmation from her family and friends, she may constantly expect and look for her mate to verbally affirm her. On one hand, this is normal and there is nothing wrong with it, but if she is not receiving it and it begins to cause arguments in the relationship, it might be a good idea for her to consider learning how to affirm herself. I understand that it means a lot to hear it from someone we value and love, but thankfully we do not have to go through life with this ever present need and unfulfilled longing when we are quite capable of giving this to ourselves. As I said before, one of the amazing things about life is that whatever we failed to get as children, be it love, acceptance, approval, affirmation, etc., we can learn to provide those things for and to ourselves as adults. We never have to hunger and thirst for someone or something outside of us and for those of us who are believers, God has also promised to fulfill these needs, holes, spaces, gaps, and voids in our lives. The truth is it is perfectly okay to like yourself, love yourself, take care of yourself, nurture yourself, pamper yourself, affirm yourself, approve of yourself, forgive yourself, acknowledge yourself, and accept yourself. This is how you begin to fill your own cup from the inside out. In my work with clients, one of the main treatment goals I set for everyone is to learn the value of self-validation, self-affirmation, self-approval, self-compassion, self-forgiveness, and self-love. I even wrote a short booklet on it called, "Seven Days to Improving Self Esteem" and each day focuses on developing and nurturing these essential ideals within oneself. I have learned that while the average person will immediately say yes when asked if they love themselves, when you begin to look closely at their lives, their choices, their decisions and their judgment, especially in the areas of their relationships, you often see a discrepancy between what people say and what they actually live.

Another thing to consider if you are feeling unfulfilled and depleted in your relationship is a two part question. A. "Is it worth it?" B. "If this were my child, my sibling or my best friend, would I advise them to stay?" I have found that many women who stay and endure unhealthy relationships and mistreatment would never advise someone they love to do the same. I have heard countless stories from abused women who have stayed and endured years of abuse say they finally decided to leave when the abuser began abusing their children. Sadly, some women still do not leave even then because when a woman does not know and understand her true worth, she will allow a man to buy her at a bargain and still feel as if he paid too much. While deep down she may be hoping and praying that her partner that she loves and values so much will reciprocate and treat her accordingly, remember that we teach people how to treat us by what we allow, tolerate, settle for and expect. If you allow mistreatment, then that is what you will receive. If you tolerate infidelity, that is what you will receive. If you settle for staying with him while he is having babies outside the relationship, then you are teaching him that he doesn't even have to use a condom while he is cheating on you. If you expect to be treated poorly because that is what you believe love to be, then that is what you will continue to attract and endure. It is amazing to me how women will minimize, rationalize, and justify a man's bad behavior in order to avoid confronting a situation or ending a relationship.

There are also those women who make excuses for a man's bad behavior by telling herself and other people such things as, "He was drunk," "I made him mad," or "He didn't mean it." Sadly, some women genuinely believe that if they stay with a man long enough, endure enough, and love him hard enough, they will change him. Please allow me to say that I am in the business of change and I witness every day how difficult it is for people to change their own thoughts, moods, habits, attitudes, and behaviors, etc., so I know that it is virtually impossible to change someone else. We may influence, inspire, motivate, and encourage someone to change, but ultimately, the decision to change is theirs to make.

Also amazing is the number of women who settle for bad treatment with the rationalization that she is trying to be nice. When did being nice become an excuse for allowing someone to lie, cheat, steal, take advantage of you, disrespect you, or call you out of your name? Recently, a close friend of mine told me that she finally realized that she is "too nice" in her relationships which often causes her to not set boundaries and limits. As a result, her relationship partners often take her for granted, call when they want, show up when it is convenient for them and disappear whenever they feel the urge. I shared with her that setting boundaries and limits with people is an indication of your worth and your value. We set limits on the things that we value such as money, jewelry, a car or some other possession. Therefore, we secure our money in a wallet or the bank, we keep jewelry in a safe place and we lock our cars and remove the keys to keep people from breaking in or driving away with them. We also set limits with the people we value, such as our children. We set limits on their behavior, how much candy they eat or when they are expected to get a job or move out of the home. We set limits to keep them safe and protected, but also to establish boundaries. Boundaries are defined as dividing lines that are used to identify and determine where something begins and where it ends. The property lines around our homes tell us and other people where our property begins and ends so that no one can just decide to build on our land or plant flowers in our yards. Wikipedia defines personal boundaries as "guidelines, rules or limits that help a person identify and establish reasonable, safe, permissible ways for other people to behave towards them." Wikipedia further explains that personal boundaries come from beliefs, opinions, attitudes, and past experiences. In short, boundaries tell people what they can and cannot do to you, what you will and will not allow and how you will or will not respond if those boundaries are crossed.

My pastor, Apostle Ron Carpenter Jr. of the Redemption World Outreach Center in Greenville, SC once did a relationship series called "Shipwrecked" which is available for purchase on the church website and on his podcast. It is also available on YouTube. Shipwrecked is easily the greatest teaching on relationships, intimacy, and boundaries I have ever heard! Apostle Ron starts out by explaining that boundaries are not walls because walls not only keep others out, they also keep you trapped inside. He goes on to speak about setting value on yourself and making people "qualify" for you. Finally, he uses scripture from the book of Ezekiel to define boundaries as he shares how the river's banks create boundaries between the water and the land that allows the river to flow and things to grow on either side. A swamp is where there is no separation between water and land and nothing grows.

To sum up this chapter on bag ladies, I want to appeal to women to do their inner work and heal the painful wounds and emotional baggage they may be carrying, remove the masks they may be wearing, let down the emotional walls and fortresses they have built to hide behind and set healthy limits, boundaries, and expectations in their relationships. I understand this work is not easy. I do it work every day, so I know the courage it takes to face up to, embrace, and own your stuff, but I also see the healing and the transformation that is possible when people begin to resolve and release years of stored up emotional pain. I encourage all bag ladies to make peace with your pasts, resolve your issues, face the giants in your lives and slay them one by one. You are worth it, and you deserve it regardless of what anyone else may have told you or shown you.

Chapter 8

Oh no! You again?

Relationship Patterns, Cycles, and Behaviors

Have you found yourself dating the same type of man over and over again? No matter how much you try to change it and date outside the box, sooner or later, the same issues begin to appear in the relationship… control issues, trust issues, commitment issues, intimacy issues, financial issues, or compatibility issues. You date older men, younger men, men from different races or ethnic backgrounds, men you meet on dating websites or through mutual friends and yet as time goes on, these seemingly different men begin to appear very familiar as you realize you are trapped in the same relationship patterns and cycles. Although the names and faces may change, you end up dealing with some of the same issues, again.

What is it that causes us to continually attract the same types of men into our lives? Sometimes it seems as if we are literally walking around with certain words stamped on our foreheads to identify and attract the kind of man we are seeking. My mom used to joke that some of the women in our family seemed to advertise for certain types of men because they ended up with the same types again and again. If you look at it from the Law of Attraction perspective, energetically, you are receiving back exactly what you are sending out. The Bible calls this the principle of sowing and reaping. Another theory is that you attract what you are and still another says you attract people based on your own needs for healing. Either way, one thing for certain is that if you are caught up in a relationship pattern or cycle, until you become fully aware of it and understand why it keeps showing up, you are bound to repeat it. I once heard a pastor say that life will keep giving us the same tests until we learn the lessons which indicate we are ready to move forward.

Let us examine how people form certain behavior and relationship patterns and why these patterns may continue to play out in their lives despite their best efforts to change them. You may have heard about girls who grew up with abusive fathers that end up dating one abusive man after the other or marrying an abusive husband? You may have known girls who grew up with mothers or fathers with substance abuse issues that either developed those issues themselves or repeatedly date partners who struggle with those issues. These are just two examples of how relationship patterns are formed, but there are many other reasons people form habits and establish patterns. As previously mentioned, sometimes people enter relationships as adults to heal "stuff" from their childhoods. So the daughter of an alcoholic father will marry an alcoholic husband who she is constantly trying to help get well when she is really subconsciously trying to heal and save her unresolved issues with "daddy." The woman who grew up without a lot of affection or emotional expression from her mother and/or father finds herself dating men who are emotionally distant, cold, and unavailable. Regardless of what your particular reasons may be or the roots of your own relationship "stuff," the key is to become aware of your tendencies, habits, and patterns so that you gain a deeper understanding into what is motivating you from within and defining your relationship patterns. This also requires you to refrain from pointing fingers at the men you keep attracting as the truth of the matter is that they are only playing out the role that you have unknowingly assigned them to play in your life. Once you begin to understand and accept the role you play and that others play in your relationship "stories," you can rewrite earlier scripts that are now outdated and give the characters in your life new parts to play. As your story changes, you may also notice that what once attracted you and turned you on no longer interests you. In fact, it may actually become a turn-off.

In this chapter, my aim is to help you learn to identify your relationship patterns and cycles so that you can become more aware of why you continue to attract certain personality and behavior types. If you truly want to break your unhealthy patterns and develop healthier new patterns that better serve you, you must be willing to face the truth, speak the truth, and live the truth or you will be bound to keep repeating the same tests. When you can be honest with yourself about your own unmet needs and unresolved issues, you can begin to heal and resolve whatever is necessary for you to start making healthier decisions and choices. Once you change your feelings, thoughts, and behaviors, everything around you will begin to change as well.

The following types and examples are not meant to categorize all men, demonize men or even bash men. As I have stated throughout this book, my belief is that all of us are responsible for the choices we make in our relationships and our lives and if we are continuing to attract the wrong men, then it is not the fault of the men, God or the universe. Even if the root of our unhealthy relationship pattern is linked to some childhood issue, as adults, the responsibility for healing and resolving those issues lies with us. Otherwise, we remain victims, and nothing in our lives gets better, except the stories we tell.

Let's explore some of the different male relationship roles and types including the women they are usually attracted to and why.

Mr. Can't Get Right

Some women will find themselves dating the guy I like to call "Mr. Can't Get Right". Mr. Can't Get Right always seems to need you for something, whether it is to build up his ego, provide him with emotional affection and support, financial assistance, physical support, or become his "mama." He brings little to the table, but expects and demands a lot and you find yourself often feeling physically, emotionally, and financially drained by the relationship rather than inspired and increased by it. You may find that you constantly pour into this guy and yet he never seems to fill up. Although he may start off with lots of promises and you may see loads of potential at the beginning of the relationship, few of his ideas and ventures ever work out, and you soon realize that most of them are just talk with very little results. Then right about the time you are fed up and have had enough, he comes through with one small thing that keeps you hanging on for a few more months or years believing he will eventually become everything you imagine and everything he has pretended to be. In the meantime, you may find yourself helping pay his child support and encouraging him to spend time with his children, helping him finish school, get a job, get his license and car tags straightened out or pay for his divorce. You may finance his business ideas, provide him with clothing, transportation, and even housing while he "gets on his feet." Mr. Can't Get Right may even have substance abuse issues, be constantly unemployed and looking for work, and is always having one financial crisis after another from which you have to bail him out. Who is he attracted to? Women who have a need to be needed and who gain a sense of purpose and self-worth from "fixing" someone in the hopes that once she fixes him, he will be so grateful to her that he will not only stay with her, but he will eventually reward her for all the good she has bestowed upon him. Mr. Can't Get Right attracts needy women, women with low self-esteem, women who fear being alone, and even Miss Independent who likes having a project. If you are continually finding yourself attracted to and dating Mr. Can't Get Right, carefully examine your internal motivations and ask yourself, "Exactly, why am I in this relationship and what do I hope to gain from it?" Do you have a need to be needed or to be in control? Weirdly, in some cases where Mr. Can't Get Right does seem to get it right and straighten out his life, he may either start to be unattracted to you or you may become unattracted to him because your roles have now changed and the unhealthy reasons that drew you together in the first place are no longer of interest to either of you. Once he becomes healthy and self-sufficient, you may then become fearful and insecure that he no longer needs you and you no longer know what role you play in his life. If you wish to break this pattern, then resolve your own stuff first so that can begin to attract and choose partners who are not dependent on you and who bring something to the relationship instead of taking away from it.

Mama's Boy

We all may remember the mama's boy from Steve Harvey's movie, Think Like a Man, played by Terrence J. Terrence J's character, Michael, and his mother had a very close relationship that we therapists like to refer to as enmeshment. According to Wikipedia, enmeshment describes a state of cross-generational bonding in a family where a child of the opposite sex becomes a surrogate mate or spouse for their parent. In the movie, Michael and his mother were so entangled with one another that he had little room for a real relationship with a woman because in essence, his mother was his woman. This began to cause numerous problems in his relationship when he had to make choices between both of the women in his life. In the end, he finally stands up to his mother and asserts his manhood. As much as I loved Michael's character in the movie and found myself laughing, the mama's boy is an everyday reality for some women and the women dating or married to mama's boys are doing anything but laughing. Being involved with a mama's boy can be frustrating as you always have to compete with his mother. Also, while the mama's boy may actually be employed and have his own home and transportation, he still may share many of the same traits as the guy who can't get right. Because of this man's "close" relationship with his mama, he may be a bit needier and more dependent on you as his woman than normal. He may constantly need you to make decisions for him or frequently advise him on major career, financial, and life decisions. You may also end up caring for most of his physical needs such as picking up after him or managing the household finances because he is unwilling or unable to do so. You may honestly at times feel like you are his mama although he will most likely resent you if you bring that to his attention.

In my professional experience in the social and human services field, I have witnessed many single mothers whose sons become the surrogate men in their lives. Their older sons are often referred to and treated as the man of the house. These sons may even help provide support for the family by working or watching the younger siblings when his mother is not home. Since most sons are naturally very protective of their mothers, he may even weigh in on his mother's romantic interests or defend her against an abusive partner if necessary. I often work to help them restructure their relationship so that these young men and boys can enjoy being children and not feel they have to be responsible for their mother's happiness.

In conclusion, dating a mama's boy can be challenging if the man is unwilling to separate, set healthy boundaries, and live his own life. One good thing about the mama's boy is that if he truly loves his mama, is respectful to her and good to her, then he will certainly know how to be good to you. If you find that you are constantly dating the mama's boy, ask yourself if you have a need to be in control. Perhaps a part of you may even enjoy him being dependent on you as this allows you to guide and direct the relationship. If your issue is not a need for control, but you love men who love their mamas, keep in mind that if this pattern has been established for a long time, then it will also take time for him to break it. Do not constantly criticize, judge or attack his mother because he will defend her and may begin to see you as the trouble maker, the drama queen, and the enemy.

The Woman Hater with Mommy Issues

Perhaps opposite the mama's boy may be the guy who inwardly hates women because of unresolved issues with his mommy. This guy may be very disrespectful towards women, have little regard for women, feel superior to women, and may publicly embarrass and devalue women. He may view women as sex objects, servants, and possessions rather than as equal partners. He may use derogatory names to describe women in general and will often vocalize his negative feelings about women. Beware of dating the woman hater, because he usually does not differentiate between the women in his life, and although he may initially praise you, he will eventually begin to see you and treat you like the other women in his life if he does not resolve his mommy issues. This guy is typically angry, argumentative, difficult to please, critical, and very judgmental. Because of his general distrust of all women, you may find yourself constantly trying to prove to him that you are different, trustworthy, and virtuous. While some of these guys may have legitimate reasons for their feelings and their mommy issues, remember it is not your job to fix that for him or to make up for his mommy's failures, mistakes, and inadequacies. Everyone is responsible for resolving their own issues and healing their own lives. So if you find that you are constantly dating the woman hater, examine your own life and try to identify what keeps attracting you to these men. Do you have a constant need to prove yourself? Do you feel inadequate or not good enough? Do you inwardly feel as if you are a bad woman due to a history of rape, abuse, or promiscuity? If any of these are true, then dedicate yourself to healing your emotional wounds so that you can identify and attract healthy partners who genuinely love women and are willing and able to love you.

The Narcissist

There was an article published in Psychology Today in 2014 that gave ten signs that you are in a relationship with a narcissist. Knowing what I know now, I wish I had read this article years ago so that I could have avoided dating a couple of narcissists in my life, but you live and learn. Let's learn to identify a narcissist so that we can avoid becoming involved with one.

The first sign that you are in a relationship with a narcissist is that he tends to dominate conversations and loves to constantly talk about himself, his concerns, and his accomplishments. You may find that you struggle with being heard in the relationship because everything revolves around him and if your beliefs and ideas do not match up to his, then they are either ignored, dismissed or corrected. The second characteristic of a narcissist is that he often interrupts you as you are speaking or talks over you, especially during arguments and disagreements. He also always brings the conversation back to his viewpoints as he has little genuine interest in hearing or understanding your point of view. The third sign is that he enjoys breaking rules and violating social norms such as waiting in lines or following traffic laws which leads to the fourth sign which is the failure to adhere to boundaries as the narcissist constantly shows little to no remorse for other people's thoughts, feelings, possessions, and physical space. The fifth sign is that he likes to make himself look good externally and places a high value on his accomplishments, status, material objects, etc., to compensate for inward feelings of inadequacy. These external things represent his false self instead of his "real self" which really feels small and insecure. The sixth sign of being in a relationship with a narcissist is that he has a high sense of entitlement and expects others to cater to him with no consideration in return and the seventh sign is that narcissists are usually very charming and persuasive and as long as they are getting what they want from you and you are fulfilling their needs and desires, they will make you feel very special and wanted. However, once they become bored or have gotten what they wanted, they will lose interest and end the relationship without a second thought. The eighth sign is that they may have a grandiose personality with an exaggerated sense of self-importance and may even have you believing that you cannot live without them. The ninth sign is that he enjoys keeping you thrown off balance emotionally as a means of remaining in control and keeping your focus and attention on him. If you fail to meet his expectations, he may get angry and throw a temper tantrum. In addition, he is extremely sensitive to criticism which may cause him to want to argue (fight) or detach from you (flight). The narcissist is also quick to judge, blame, and criticize you, and he can be emotionally and physically abusive. He likes to make you feel inferior so that he can feel superior. The tenth and final sign that you may be in a relationship with a narcissist is that he will use you and others to meet his own unrealized dreams and to cover his flaws.

Now that you understand the narcissistic man's characteristics and personality, let's explore the types of women who tend to attract and date them. Typically, narcissists like to date women who are gullible and passive with low self-esteem and self-worth. They also tend to date women who have little emotional support by way of friends and family. If a woman does have emotional support, the narcissist will slowly and methodically work to alienate her from that support. The other thing about narcissists is that they are rarely interested in changing their behaviors because in their minds, they are not the ones with the problem. The narcissistic man is more interested in changing you than he is in changing himself. This is not to say that they cannot change. I am in the business of change, so I know that change is possible, but you may spend a lot of time investing in and nurturing this type of man long before you begin to see any positive changes in him and you may find yourself feeling mentally, emotionally, and spiritually exhausted in the process. Many women have become involved with narcissists without even realizing it until they are deep in the relationship and emotionally involved as narcissists are very persuasive and charming and initially may appear to have all the right attributes. They may be high-powered, successful men that dress well, speak well and make great impressions on friends and family members. However, not all narcissists are successful. Some of them are unemployed, incarcerated, domestic abusers, substance abusers, rapists, and even serial killers. Again, he may be very hard to detect initially, but you will soon begin to see his other side as the relationship progresses. Because he is a master at manipulation, you may even question or blame yourself for the issues in the relationship. Picture the character Carlos in the Tyler Perry movie, Madea's Family Reunion.

He was a handsome, successful investment banker who was physically and emotionally abusive behind closed doors and he often blamed her for his behavior.

Once you discover you are involved with a narcissist, you may find it difficult to leave and end the relationship. When you finally do leave, if he hasn't left you first, you may initially blame yourself or constantly question what you did wrong or what is wrong with you. As you begin to heal from this relationship pattern and become fully aware of how and why you were attracted to him in the first place, you will eventually start to feel relieved that you are no longer with someone who requires that level of sacrifice. As you learn to focus on your own needs and wants again, hopefully you will come to realize and accept that "love ain't that damn hard!"

The Control Freak

While the control freak and the narcissist may be one and the same, you can also date someone who is controlling, yet doesn't have the other characteristics of narcissism. Some similarities may include dominating conversations and arguments and the need to over-compensate for internal feelings of inadequacy and inferiority, but a control freak may genuinely be able to care about another person's feelings. He may also be able to express love, appreciation and affection, he just needs to be and likes to be in control. It could come from the fact that he was raised to believe that men are supposed to be in charge and that women are supposed to be subservient to them. After all, the Bible even stipulates that the man is the head of the household. However, some men fail to realize that the Bible doesn't end there. As the head of the household, not only does the man have certain rights and privileges, he also has certain responsibilities to his family. Many men have taken this passage out of context and used it as an excuse to control their spouses and families. If a man truly understands his role and his position, he won't have a need to fight for it or lord over others in order to prove himself.

Other controlling men may be that way because of what they observed as children from their own fathers and mothers. Remember, we often emulate what we see, so if a man grew up believing that men are superior and dominant, then he may honestly believe this is how men should interact and behave. In many cases, controlling men are covering up feelings of insecurity, inferiority and fear, and his need for control might be his way of trying to resolve those feelings in order to feel safe and secure. Controlling men may also be jealous and possessive which again suggests underlying feelings of insecurity and inadequacy. Whenever I work with men or women with control issues, I always try to identify and explore the underlying issues beneath the need for control as I work to educate them on the difference between power and control. Once people begin to own and accept their own innate personal power, they have less of a need to dominate and control others. So, what woman is the control freak attracted to? Similar to the narcissist, the control freak is attracted to women with low self-esteem, troubled pasts, low education, little or no financial means of support, or inadequate emotional support from friends and family. If there is an adequate amount of emotional support, he may also try to alienate her from them so that he can exert his control and authority without interference. One thing I have come to realize is that some women may honestly seek out controlling men because they are subconsciously seeking a father figure, i.e. the fatherless daughters we discussed earlier. I believe in many ways, we are all seeking to heal our unresolved childhood issues through our adult relationships. If this is you, the woman who attracts and dates controlling men, focus on improving your self-image (the way you see yourself), your self-worth (the way you value yourself), your self-esteem (the way you feel about yourself), and your self-love so that you can attract and date men who treat you the way you deserve to be treated.

The Abuser

In this section, I am going to focus on men who are physically, verbally, sexually, mentally, and emotionally abusive. Most women who have been in the dating game have undoubtedly at one time or another been involved with an abusive partner. Abusers may start out being very charming, persuasive, and seemingly too good to be true. Afraid that you may leave if he shows you who he really is in the very beginning, he pretends to be someone he is not until you have become sexually and/or emotionally involved. Although the abuser is a master concealer, there are always telltale signs. Abusers can be controlling, narcissistic, jealous and are usually very emotionally insecure. They may have mommy issues or daddy issues and typically harbor lots of anger and resentment towards other people and life in general. The verbal abuser talks down to you, criticizes you, demeans you, belittles you, and may even name-calls during arguments. Because of his own inner feelings of inferiority, he has a need to demean you so that he can feel more confident and secure.

The emotional abuser operates in much the same way although he likes to play emotional games such as breaking off the relationship only to call a few days later to say he was joking and wants to reconcile or starting frivolous arguments so that he can test your love for him. The emotional abuser also will punish you by withholding his affection if he becomes angry or disappointed with you in some way.

The mental abuser plays games with your mind, your self-esteem and your self-image. His goal is to change the way you think about yourself, see yourself, and feel about yourself. If you have high self-esteem or high self-worth, his desire is to bring you down to his level so that he can feel less inferior. He is also manipulative, conniving, and deceptive.

The physical abuser starts out with slight displays of aggressive behavior such as getting up in your face, pushing you, or grabbing your arm too hard before he actually begins to hit you. Once he does begin hitting you, he will initially apologize, buy you gifts, and do his best to keep you from leaving. As you begin to settle for this behavior and become more tolerant of it, he may convince you that his hitting you is in reaction to something you do or fail to do. Eventually, he will offer no explanation, justification, or apology for his actions.

The sexual abuser in terms of adult relationships is somewhat different from sexual abusers of children. The sexual abuser in an adult relationship is sexually aggressive, demanding, and may resort to forcing his partner into having sex if he is denied affection. He also sees nothing wrong with his actions and feels a sense of entitlement based on his manhood and his expectations in the relationship.

If you are dating abusive men over and over again, perhaps you have a personal history of sexual, physical, verbal or emotional abuse, and you feel that this is what love looks and feels like. Or perhaps you were emotionally neglected and have a low sense of self-worth which causes you to think you do not deserve any better. Either way, you are mistaken and I would strongly advise you to do your inner work to become healthy and whole. You do deserve better, not all men are abusive, and love does not hurt.

The Emotionally Unavailable Guy

Have you repeatedly found yourself in relationships with guys who are unwilling or unable to show affection, express their true feelings, and engage in genuine emotional intimacy? If so, you may be dating the emotionally unavailable guy (EUG). This guy, sometimes for reasons unknown, is the guy who rarely gives you compliments, encouragement or praise. He shows little to no emotion at times when you are at your most vulnerable such as during the death of a loved one or during a setback or disappointment. On the flipside, he may also be unable or unwilling to help you celebrate joyous occasions such as promotions, achievements or other special events. The EUG rarely shows affection outside of intercourse in the way of hugging, kissing or other intimate touching and he has no idea how to create or initiate genuine intimacy. Now do not get this guy confused with men who simply have a different love language than yours. Many of us are familiar with Dr. Gary Chapman's book, "The Five Love Languages." If not, I highly recommend reading it and discovering your own individual love language and your man's love language. You can also go online and fill out the questionnaire.

According to Dr. Chapman, we all have different ways of expressing our love and affection. My love language is "Words of Affirmation" and my husband's love language is "Acts of Service." Before determining that you are dating an EUG, be sure that you are not simply misreading your man's love language and expecting him to know and speak your love language. Also keep in mind that some men are just naturally more affectionate than others, so be careful not to unfairly compare your man to them. The EUG is a step beyond the guy who just speaks a different love language. He may genuinely lack the ability or the desire to be available for you emotionally. He may not even be connected to his own feelings and emotions and he often struggles with expressing his emotions. Loving this guy can feel like a never-ending stream of unmet expectations, hurt feelings, and passion-less romance. If you are the type of woman who thrives on and needs outward expressions of love and affection, then you may need to rethink dating an EUG. Other women who date them may be women who grew up with a parent who was emotionally unavailable and as a result, you attract men who are just like them despite your need for emotional intimacy and encouragement. Again, heal your own stuff so you can attract someone who can and will give you the emotional support and encouragement you need and want.

The Commitment Phobe

Are you constantly dating men who cannot and will not commit? The commitment phobic man likes to take things slow, and he likes to keep things lukewarm to avoid becoming too involved or having you get too involved. This man often has internal fears of rejection and abandonment or mommy or daddy issues which may cause him to be afraid of getting close to people for fear that he will be rejected, disappointed or abandoned. The commitment phobe may also still be carrying baggage from previous relationships that he constantly reminds you of to explain and justify why he is taking things slow and failing to commit. A commitment phobe may get involved in a relationship with you, date you for years, but will be hesitant and even resistant to taking that relationship farther. He may decide to move in and live with you, but again with little real commitment. This man likes having the option to get out quickly if necessary and he always has a plan "B." Similar to dating the EUG, dating a commitment phobe can be emotionally draining and frustrating as you may invest years of your time, your emotions, and your life into this guy without ever reaping any benefit from it or seeing any progress. Women who typically date commitment phobes may have commitment issues of their own and are subconsciously sabotaging themselves without even realizing it. If you have your own unresolved mommy and daddy issues of rejection and abandonment, you may be inwardly avoiding real intimacy and commitment yourself. Since it is far more difficult to identify your own motivations for being in the relationship, you make yourself feel better by blaming things on the commitment phobic man as the reason the relationship has not progressed. Heal your own stuff and resolve your own issues so you can feel safe and secure in attaching to and committing to men who are also available and willing to commit.

The Player

This is the character Zeke in "Think Like a Man." The player, ladies' man, womanizer, or whatever name you wish to call him definitely makes our list of the type of guy you may be constantly be attracting into your life. As you may have guessed, the player and the commitment phobic have a lot in common. The player is also not likely to be interested in settling down and making long term commitments. Some men genuinely feel monogamy is unnatural and believe that it is in a man's nature to explore and date a variety of women and truly seem to enjoy the attention and affections of more than one woman. If you are constantly dating the player, understand that he usually has no desire to settle down with one woman and you may be wasting your time trying to "catch" him or convince him that you are the one. Assess whether you have your own commitment issues or whether you witnessed this behavior from either of your parents during your childhood. Also, if you struggle with a poor self-image, low self-esteem and self-worth, you may find yourself dating men who do not see the value in committing to you. Because they are usually quite charming with a lot of swag, you may find yourself already sexually or emotionally involved with him before you find out who he really is, but then you will need to decide if it is worth to spend the rest of your life trying to change him. Players do settle down sometimes, but usually, it is when they make that decision themselves, not when you need or want him to. So if you are attracted to this guy and you truly desire to be in a committed, monogamous relationship, know what you are getting yourself into and think long and hard about whether you mind sharing him and also whether you have the time or the patience to see if he will change.

Married, Separated or Otherwise Attached Man

Sadly, some married men also fit in the player category. I like to call them "single husbands". Single husbands are men who are legally married, but date and operate as if they are single. These men do not honor their commitment to their wives and will gladly carry on extramarital relationships with women who are willing to be the side chick. The single husband may or may not make promises of leaving his spouse to be with you. He will, however, justify why he does what he does. He may claim that his spouse doesn't understand him the way you do. He may claim that he and his wife are no longer intimate and he has physical and sexual needs to fulfill. He may also tell you that the marriage is over, but he is staying around for his children. Finally, he may simply lie and deceive you until you are emotionally involved with him before he even reveals to you his marital status. I understand that some women may have already become involved with married men before finding out, and then find it difficult to leave. This is another great reason for taking your time to really get to know someone while being on the lookout for those little red flags. Does he disappear at night? Does he go missing for days at a time? Does he ignore phone calls or walk outside to accept them? These may all be tell-tale signs that there is someone else.

Prior to my getting married, I had a rule against dating married or otherwise attached men. While I certainly knew other women who dated them on a regular basis, I refrained for a couple of reasons. The first reason was

114

that I did not want that bad karma returning to me if and when I ever did get married. Secondly, I had been hurt myself by someone cheating on me, and I never wanted to knowingly cause that pain to another person. I would not even date men who claimed to be separated from their wives because I considered that to be unfinished business. Amazingly, because of my commitment and resolve not to date married men, I was rarely approached by them. My friends would tell countless stories of being hit on by married men, and I wondered what was different about me. Did I just not appeal to them or was it something else? I later came to believe that married men can detect the type of women who will become involved with them and because I was never willing to be that woman, I simply did not interest or attract them, nor did they interest or attract me.

In addition to the men who may be married, there are also the men who are not legally married, but in a long term committed relationship or living with someone. These men usually have similar reasons to justify their actions of not being faithful to their partners. If you find that you have a pattern of attracting and dating married or otherwise attached men, ask yourself if you have a fear of commitment and inwardly feel that by dating someone who is not really available keeps you from having to face that fear. You could also be one of the women who is convinced that the married man is better off with you and you may believe everything he is telling you about his marriage and his wife. You may even sympathize with him. One thing I have learned about men is that you cannot make a man do anything he does not want to do.

Therefore, if a married or attached man is that unhappy and dissatisfied, there isn't a woman on earth who can make him stay. If he is still there, it is usually because he either wants to be there or doesn't have enough onus to leave yet. Either way, you are risking a lifetime of hurt, loneliness, broken promises, broken heartedness, and bad karma in addition to being at risk of an unwanted pregnancy or sexually transmitted disease.

Bad Boys

I remember when I went through my own phase of dating "bad boys." All my life, I had dated the seemingly "good guys" who were employed and educated. Men who looked good on paper and seemed to be good catches, yet I could not seem to "catch" one I wanted to hold onto or one who wanted to hold onto me. So at around age 32, I developed this attraction to bad boys. It was just something about them that was different, and I liked it! I'm not sure if it was their "swag," their confidence or even cockiness, their bad boy persona, or their "I don't give a f*** mentality." Whatever it was, I was intrigued. My family and friends were a bit surprised by my new interests, but all I knew was that I had tried playing it safe and that had not worked out for me either. I wanted to do something different... "Lil Wayne Different." Many women will admit that there is something about bad boys that is mysterious, intriguing, sexy, and even a bit dangerous that we find attractive. I believe some of us like to think that we can change them or that we are going to be the one woman who makes them settle down and get on the straight and narrow. Others may see the bad boy as a project, someone to fix and repair. Perhaps it goes back to the whole fairytale notion of being rescued by a brave knight on a white horse, or maybe it speaks to our need for safety and protection, something we may have needed as children and did not receive from our fathers. However, the truth is that sometimes we are actually putting ourselves in danger when we are with bad boys, especially those involved in illegal activities.

My husband and I love the show "For My Man" which airs on TV One. This show chronicles the lives of young girls and women who sacrifice their children, their freedom and even their lives for the men they love. What is interesting to me is that in many of the stories, the women have only known these guys for a very short time. Story after story, we see these girls and women committing heinous crimes from armed robbery to cold-blooded murder. For their involvement, a lot of them end up getting sentenced to life in prison without parole and even death. In my opinion, no relationship should require that level of sacrifice.

Author and poet, Asha Bandele, wrote a book called "The Prisoner's Wife", which is an excellently written memoir of her life and marriage to her incarcerated husband, Rashid. In the book, Asha describes in detail the challenges of being married to an inmate, living alone and raising their child alone on the outside. The reason I mentioned that book is because of the women I know personally and professionally who have met, dated, married, and waited for men who were and are still incarcerated and I have seen the toll it takes on them and their children. Some of these men have life sentences, and yet these women have made the choice to remain committed to relationships with men they may not even be married to. Sadly, when some of the men are released, they end up abandoning the very women who have waited so patiently for them, or they end up being released into the custody of other women with whom they have also been communicating with while they were locked up.

So if you like the bad boy swag, attitude, and lifestyle, go for it. Just be sure you understand what you may be signing up for as all of us have to make the relationship choices that closely match the vision we have for our lives.

I am still not sure what it was for me other than being fed up with dating conventional guys who lied, deceived, cheated, and mistreated me. I think I also appreciated the fact that bad boys seemed to be very straightforward and brutally honest. However, I soon learned that they also lied, deceived, cheated, and mistreated women. I recall my mother once saying you can't change a street person. You can dress them up and fix them up, but in the end, they go right back to being who they really are. There are women I know who constantly date bad boys and go through tons of baby mama drama, infidelity, disappointment, and heartache. That is not to say that all bad boys are bad people. In fact, I know several men who have simply gotten caught up in circumstances that caused them to make choices and decisions that had negative life changing consequences. Thankfully for me, I eventually outgrew my bad boy phase and married a good guy who is far from perfect, but perfect for me, our children, and the life I envisioned.

The Addict

While this may be the last category I discuss in this chapter, this is in no way an exhaustive or complete analysis of the different relationship patterns, cycles, and types, but I have attempted to capture the most common.

One of the most challenging men you may find yourself continually dating or married to is the alcoholic and/or drug addict. As a professional psychotherapist, I decided not to treat substance abuse in my practice. The main reason is that I like having a frame of reference when I work with clients and since I really do not have any addictions myself (other than shoes and sugar), the truth is that I have never experienced the cravings of an alcoholic or drug addict, nor the physiological need for a particular substance. I love a good margarita, but if I was never able to drink one again in life, I would be just fine. That is not necessarily true for the addict or substance abuser. Once their use of a substance becomes dependence and abusive, they not only have a mental desire for that substance, they have a physical need for it as well. According to my mother, my father became an alcoholic later in their marriage, and she often talked about the difference in his personality before he became an alcoholic and afterwards. She talked about the drastic changes in his mood and behavior, something that is common to substance abusers. While I have no memory of any of this, I am aware of the tendency for children of alcoholics or substance abusers to either end up using themselves or become involved with users. I vowed not to repeat that pattern, and although I have dated the weed smoker and the social drinker, I have never been attracted to habitual drug users and abusers. It is a turn off for me and a deal breaker. Some women may find themselves continually attracting and dating men with substance abuse issues because of their own personal experiences. I did not grow up in a home where my mother was always partying, and although my father was an alcoholic, I can count how many times I ever saw my mother actually drink and she never used any drugs.

Through my education and experience in this field, I have grown to understand substance abusers and the effects that drugs and alcohol can have on them personally as well as their children, partners, and families. I also treat a lot of adults with chronic anxiety and depression who grew up in homes with substance abusers. Because of the volatility of the substance abuser, children raised in those types of homes tend to grow up with a lot of emotional issues. Many end up using themselves while others end up dating and marrying someone similar to their abusive parent(s).

If you are involved with a substance abuser, please know that addicts tend to be cunning, manipulative, and deceitful, and their relationships are often violent, unpredictable and mentally, emotionally, and financially draining on their friends and loved ones. Many incidents of domestic and interpersonal violence are also closely linked to drug use and intoxication. Women who attract and date addicts are usually struggling with issues of codependency, low self-esteem and self-worth, and poor boundaries.

Substance abuse can be a very hard cycle to break, but it can be broken, and many alcoholics and drug addicts go on to live sober, drug-free lives. There are many agencies and support groups out there who provide education, insight, counseling, and assistance to people struggling with substance abuse and the families affected by it. Do not be afraid to reach out if you need help. If the abuser is unwilling to get help and you are not married, you may need to rethink whether the relationship is worth it. If you are married, remember that you are in covenant agreement with that person and it won't be as easy to walk away. I would recommend you examine and explore every possible solution including prayer, fasting, pastoral counseling, couple's therapy, etc. In the end, you still may have to decide whether it is worth it to stay. Every relationship we engage in either adds to our lives or subtracts from it. You determine which. Regardless of whether or not the abuser gets help, you can get help for yourself and any children who might be involved so that you can begin to break this unhealthy pattern and cycle for you and for them.

In closing, I hope this chapter on relationship roles, habits, patterns, cycles, and behaviors has not given you the impression that all men fall or fit into one of these categories. I believe and know that there are good men out there who are excellent fathers, mates, and husbands, and I am happily married to one myself. I once heard someone say that sometimes on the road to meeting your prince charming, you may meet and kiss a few frogs along the way. Our bad relationship experiences are not there to make us believe that we do not deserve to be loved, that we will never find a good man or that we simply are not good enough and will have to settle. I believe the bad experiences are there to help us clearly define who we are, what we deserve, what we are worth, what we want, don't want, and what we can tolerate, live with, and endure.

Part II

Finding the Love You Want & Deserve

The first part of this book has hopefully given you loads of information, practical and theoretical knowledge, personal and professional experiences, and valuable insight that will help you better understand your past and current relationship choices, decisions, cycles, patterns, beliefs, and behaviors. Relationships are not easy. Even the good ones require work, dedication, patience, understanding, selflessness, and forgiveness. It is an ongoing process, as is all of life. Once you do meet and connect with a good man, remember that is not where the work ends. In some ways, this is when the real work begins because you have to maintain what you have. Many relationships can start out one way and become completely different as the people begin to grow and change. The reality is that no one is perfect and I constantly remind people that there will be work involved in every relationship and you will always have to put up with something. The key is knowing and defining your deal breakers. I have come to learn that just as we go through changes and phases as individuals, so do our relationships. None of us are who we were five years ago. While we may be repeating the same actions, or having similar experiences, other things about us have undoubtedly changed such as our weight, our perspectives, our hair, or our financial situations. On a cellular level, none of us are who we were even twenty-four hours ago. Change is an inevitable part of life, and if a relationship is going to last, you best believe there will be some changes, hardships, trials and tribulations. This is the basis and foundation of commitment. It means sticking it out, seeing it through and remembering to forgive, love and laugh along the way. If you are going to attract and maintain a lasting healthy relationship, there will be some changes you may be required to make before that relationship and during the course of that relationship.

In my own journey, I had to make several changes within myself so that I could attract a healthy mate. A few years before I met my husband, I asked God to send me a mate who would love me half as much as He loved me and I wrote down a list of the qualities I wanted him to possess. I prayed over that list and put it underneath my mattress. I then asked God to mold me and teach me to be the type of woman who would attract the type of man I was seeking. At the time, I didn't know what I was fully committing to. I didn't know that I was going to have to be broken down spiritually and emotionally so that I could truthfully see myself as I was, take ownership of my stuff (the good and the bad), admit what wasn't working and transform my life and my relationships with God, with men and with myself. I had to learn the true value of who I was as a woman and embrace my femininity without fear of being vulnerable or weak. I learned the true meaning of submission and how to let a man be a man. I also had to forgive the men in my past, including my daddy and I had to stop seeing all men as my enemy. I even had to change the ways I referred to men. I clearly remember one day realizing that I could not continue praying for God to send my prince charming while I was still calling men "dogs." I began to deliberately seek out examples of what I perceived to be good men, good fathers, and good husbands, and I questioned them on the qualities they looked for in a woman. I also observed how they treated their women and their children. Slowly, my perceptions began to shift. I began to have a better understanding of what I should expect, what I should tolerate, and what I should be willing to reciprocate. I had to discover and define what I was worth, what I deserved and what I expected. I also had to become who and what I wanted to attract.

As you read part two, hopefully, you will learn some things you can begin doing to change your thoughts, habits, feelings, beliefs, and behaviors in regards to men, yourself and your relationships. By accepting responsibility for your actions and addressing your need for healing or simply changing the ways you view men, love, marriage and relationships, you too will begin changing the course of love in your life.

Chapter 9

Cleaning House

Throughout this book, I have focused on the woman's need for self-awareness, responsibility, accountability, and healing. This chapter on cleaning house will take those lessons one step further by helping you learn to forgive yourself and others, sever ungodly and unhealthy soul ties, break unhealthy relationship habits and patterns, clear your emotional baggage, detox between relationships, destroy past relationship vows, covenants and agreements, and even clear out your physical clutter and why these things are critical to healthy relationships.

Forgiveness

Most of us are familiar with the concept of forgiveness, yet many of us still do not fully understand how to do it or even why it is necessary, but in order for you to move forward and have healthy relationships, you must become willing to forgive everybody in your past for everything. I understand this is easier said than done as I too have struggled with forgiveness. Like many people, I felt that forgiving someone meant condoning what they had done to me or allowing them to get away with what they had done to me. I had been through some really bad experiences in my life, so the thought of forgiving those people who had wronged me was one of the hardest challenges I ever had to face. Sometimes I still have to remind myself of the importance of forgiveness, from a practical and a spiritual perspective. Forgiveness is not easy, and it may not be a one-time event. We can all say the words, but until there is a genuine shift in our hearts, we may not be done with the process. I have read forgiveness prayers aloud, prayed at the altar, and even fasted only to be reminded that my feelings really had not changed when I saw the person or remembered the infraction. Some people are naturally very forgiving. Several of my close friends are that way, and even though I admire that about them now, at one time I thought they were being pushovers who were allowing people to take advantage of them. I still feel that people sometimes use forgiveness as an excuse to continue on in the same circumstances or continue putting up with the same undesirable behavior. For example, if someone cheats on you repeatedly, you may forgive them, but that does not mean you have to stay involved with them. What I have learned about forgiveness is that it is an act of courage and will, not a passive response or excuse to overlook bad behavior. Forgiving a person may actually require you to end a friendship or relationship with someone while letting go of the hurt, anger, disappointment, bitterness, and resentment. From a practical perspective, unforgiveness has been described as drinking poison while expecting another person to die. It is punishing yourself by holding onto negative emotions and experiences caused by someone else. It is like hitting yourself and expecting someone else to say ouch! The sad truth is that many times the people we have not forgiven have gone on with their lives and not given us a second thought.

Perhaps one of the hardest people to forgive is someone who continues to wound you such as close family members. It may not always be easy to cut someone off or walk away when you are in close relationship with them. I can remember justifying my own unwillingness to forgive by telling myself that forgiving someone who kept offending me was giving them permission to keep doing it. What I now know is that people are sometimes acting out their own stuff on you and their attacks have more to do with who they are or where they are in life than it has to do with you. That is not an excuse for their behavior or mistreatment, but it keeps us from allowing their external attacks to cause internal damage inside of us. The Bible says that out of the heart flows the issues of life. I like to say, "Out of the heart, the mouth speaks." So when someone continues attacking you or offending you, remember that it is more of an indication of who they are than it is an accurate assessment of who you are. How do you deal with them then if you have chosen not to disengage or end the relationship? You can keep forgiving them and try to separate the person from their behavior. You can also have a discussion with them about your expectations and set firm limits and boundaries regarding what you will and will not allow and tolerate. In the end, you may end up limiting the frequency of your contact with them or learning to love them from a distance.

Forgiveness is also a spiritual concept. God forgives us and expects us to forgive the people who have transgressed against us. He also advises us to forgive our debtors because He has forgiven our debts. The Bible goes on to say that if we refuse to forgive others, God may refuse to forgive us. My research has also revealed that unforgiveness may actually block our blessings and our happiness. Not because God is withholding those things from us, but because unforgiveness usually leads to hard-heartedness and hard-heartedness creates a wall around our hearts that keeps people and things from getting in. This wall not only blocks the bad stuff, but it also blocks the good. Unforgiveness is like building a prison to keep someone else locked in without realizing that we are being imprisoned as well. I often tell my clients, someone has to be there to keep the gates locked. Whoever has wounded you, hurt you, taken advantage of you, abused you, lied to you, deceived you, and betrayed you has already done enough damage. Do not allow them to continue having power over you as you continue to damage and punish yourself for something they have done. Release them and let them go and claim your emotional freedom and deliverance. Remember, when you don't forgive, you are agreeing to continue carrying around emotional baggage and this can and will affect your interpersonal relationships.

In this section on forgiveness, I also want to explore the need for self-forgiveness as sometimes we are more willing to forgive others than we are ourselves. People will release the feelings of anger, resentment, bitterness, and blame towards people who hurt them, but continue to beat up on themselves. We blame ourselves when people betray us. We blame ourselves when people abandon or reject us. We blame ourselves when people deceive us or disappoint us. We blame ourselves when people hurt us. We even blame ourselves for loving and trusting someone who turns out not to be who they said they were and who we believed them to be. I have counseled clients who are still blaming themselves for believing in someone that they loved and trusted. I always remind them that sometimes you can't help who you love, and loving someone is not wrong in and of itself. If someone you loved and trusted is unable to appreciate that, respect it and reciprocate it, it is their loss. Sometimes people are doing us a favor when they leave our lives even if we do not feel that way or recognize it at the time because being attached to the wrong person will slowly destroy your happiness and peace of mind.

Maybe your unforgiveness of yourself is not about what other people have done to you, but what you have done to them or to yourself. Perhaps you are still holding onto past mistakes you have made, bad decisions, and poor choices. Either way, be willing to accept responsibility for those things and move on. God can and will forgive all of our sins and erase all of our debts. Not only that, He promises that as far as east is from west, He will no longer even remember them. Surely if God can do that, you can find a way to forgive yourself. The truth is, unforgiveness towards ex-boyfriends, ex-husbands, past partners, and baby daddies can and will affect our current and future relationships and that past emotional baggage will keep showing up to interfere in your life and rob you of your present joy. Clean house and let it go. Consider the following examples. When you owe a debt for your house, car or credit card and you finally pay that debt off, you do not send that company a payment the following month "just because." You accept that the debt is paid in full and you move on with your life. Likewise, if a food or drink has gone past its expiration date, you get rid of it. It has outlived its usefulness and is no longer healthy or necessary. Finally, when prisoners have served their time and the parole board or judge issues a release date, not one of them shows up the following week for count.

In conclusion, no matter what someone has done to you or you may have done to yourself in your past relationships, give those debts, transgressions, sins, and offenses an expiration date, a release date and a paid in full date so that you can wipe the slate clean and live fully in the present.

Severing un-Godly and unhealthy soul ties

The next area of your house that may need cleaning is the presence of ungodly and unhealthy soul ties and attachments. I mentioned the issue of soul ties in the chapter on sex because most often this is how and when unhealthy soul ties are formed. However, they can also be formed in other ways. Because most soul ties occur during sexual intercourse, you are most likely still connected to anyone and everyone you have had sex with outside of marriage. This connection and attachment can and will show up in your present relationship. Since soul ties can also create entry points into your body and your life, you always want to sever them once a relationship has ended, especially if that relationship was unhealthy, abusive, or ungodly. Even if the relationship was somewhat healthy or happy and ended for other reasons, it is still good practice to sever any ties with that person to ensure that you are whole and complete for your current and future partners. Otherwise, you risk having pieces of yourself still entangled with past lovers.

Have you ever felt like you just could not stop thinking about someone from your past even though the relationship has been over for years? If so, there may be an existing soul tie or attachment that has not been severed. Because you and your new partner deserve for you to be fully present in your current relationship, make sure you sever any ties and attachments from the past. Severing soul ties is a spiritual process and may require the assistance of a spiritual leader, so do not approach this process lightly nor underestimate the need for it. In the end, you may be surprised to discover who you are still attached to and why they continue to have an effect on you.

For those of you who are not believers and wish to discredit this section on soul ties, make sure you read and gain an understanding of the power of energetic cords and attachments between people and things because the premise is pretty much the same. For example, if you have ever thought of someone seconds before they called you or you were about to call them, that usually indicates the presence of an energetic attachment. Make a list of past lovers or former friends with whom you may be spiritually or energetically attached to and develop a plan to sever those ties that no longer serve you.

Detoxing between relationships

Along with severing past soul ties, it is also important that you detox between relationships. Because some women have fears of rejection, abandonment and being alone, they may find themselves going from relationship to relationship without ever fully disengaging and detoxifying from the previous one. We are all familiar with the benefits of a physical detox. A good physical detox may help us to lose excess weight, increase our energy, become more focused and clear in our thinking, reduce belly bloating and gain a renewed sense of purpose in life. I remember the first time I did the 10-Day Green Smoothie Cleanse by JJ Smith. (If you are not familiar with this cleanse, please visit her page on Facebook and buy her book!) I had planned to start the cleanse on New Year's Day 2014. The day before I was to begin, I started coming up with all sorts of reasons as to why I should wait when my husband walks in the house carrying all of the ingredients I would need for the first five days. At that moment, I knew I had to at least start the cleanse and make a valiant effort to complete it. I remember that the first four days were the hardest for me. I was hungry, irritable, and I felt deprived, so I began to tell myself all the reasons why it was okay for me to quit. Thankfully, the book had indicated that the first four days would be the toughest and that if we could make it to days five and six, then the cleanse would get easier. So as hard as it was, I decided to stick it out. I also enlisted encouragement from my support system who continued to motivate me to keep going. Around day six or seven, I began to gain this amazing sense of clarity. I also noticed my skin had this healthy, youthful glow and my belly was much flatter as well. For the first time since having my daughter the previous year via emergency c-section, I could button my tight jeans without feeling like I was about to pass out. This gave me the confidence I needed to go ahead and finish the last four days. On the tenth day, my family and I went shopping, and I actually did not feel deprived when they stopped to eat at the food court. Instead, I felt focused, determined, and renewed. Once I completed the full ten day cleanse, I continued to do the modified version for another ten to fifteen days and have done the modified version at different intervals since then. In all, I lost about sixteen pounds, but that was not what impressed me the most. What I recall most vividly was that I felt absolutely amazing, physically, mentally, emotionally and spiritually! This cleanse which started off being a way to jumpstart my weight loss for the new year had ended up helping me detox in so many other ways.

I have now come to believe that we can all benefit from detoxing. A mental and emotional detox, especially in between relationships, can help us to allow ourselves space and time to heal so that we do not drag any old emotional baggage into a new relationship. Taking time for an emotional and mental detox also allows us to reflect on past decisions, behaviors, and the lessons we learned so that we can continue to grow, develop, and expand. It will also help us to identify and sever those past soul ties so that we can be fully restored to the present, whole and complete.

Breaking past relationship vows, covenants, and agreements

Since you are now aware of the importance of severing soul ties and detoxing between relationships, another thing you may want to consider is breaking any past relationship vows, covenants, and agreements. Relationship vows, covenants, and agreements are similar to marriage vows and covenants or custody agreements except that there may be no legal ramifications for breaking them. Relationship vows, covenants, and agreements can be spoken aloud such as vowing to love someone forever or they may be implied such as wearing a promise ring or engagement ring. You may have verbally ended a relationship, but physically you may still be in a covenant agreement with that person by allowing them to keep a key to your home or by holding onto their clothing and other belongings after the relationship has ended. Take some time to reflect on whether you are maintaining any covenants, agreements or vows with someone so that you can make a plan to break them and move forward. This may require verbally breaking the agreement aloud or returning the person's possessions. Prior to getting married to my husband, I went through all of the old gifts I had received over the years from previous boyfriends and began ridding myself of them. I gave some things away to family and friends and donated other items to charity. You are not required to do this, but it is what I chose to do for me because I wanted nothing from my past to interfere with my current and future happiness.

Clearing Physical Clutter

All things are comprised of energy, even inanimate objects such as jewelry and clothing, and if a vow, covenant or agreement is attached to an item, then it carries even more weight and has greater significance. Therefore, in addition to doing forgiveness work, severing soul ties, and detoxing between relationships, you may need to physically clear the clutter in your next phase of house cleaning. This may involve releasing items of emotional or sentimental value. Any jewelry, clothing, furniture or other item purchased by an ex-partner is a potential tie and attachment to that person, and it may benefit you greatly to let it go. Whether you believe it or not, holding onto these things is a sign that you are not yet ready to move forward. Although you may love the item, feel you've earned it, need it and feel attached to it, these items have the ability to maintain energetic cords and attachments. Also, when you become involved in a new relationship, no man wants to think about you holding onto reminders of your past relationship.

Another reason it is important to clean house and clear physical clutter is that you must create a space for a healthy partner to fill. Holding onto past junk clutters that space and can literally block your blessings. You may be familiar with the scripture in Matthew 9:17 that says, "Neither do people pour new wine into old wineskins. If they do, the skins burst; the wine will run out and the wineskins will be ruined. No, they pour new wine into new wineskins, and both are preserved." This parable can be applied to relationships and other areas of your life. You must clear out the old to make way for the new. This is one of the reasons why some people struggle to make positive affirmations work in their lives. You have to clear the faulty belief in order to create space for the new belief.

I realized the true value of this in my own life about eight years ago before my husband and I became pregnant with my son. We had not been using any protection and yet I had not conceived. According to my doctors, there was nothing physically wrong with either of us, so we were confused as to what was preventing our conception. Then one day I was reading a book on spiritual prosperity while sitting under the dryer in the hair salon. I had come to a section in the book where it was talking about how clutter blocks our blessings. It even stated that having your money in disarray in your wallet prevents new money from flowing in. As I sat there, all of a sudden I was struck with a deep revelation that seemed to come from nowhere as I realized that I had not been able to conceive presently because I was still holding onto the belongings from the baby I had lost eight years prior.

When I was twenty-eight years old, I was engaged to a guy I had known for two years and we were expecting a son. Two weeks before my due date, we discovered that our unborn son had a condition called Trisomy 18 and would most likely be stillborn or die shortly after birth. Up until that time, all of our obstetric visits had gone well, and the doctors had expressed no concern. Two days after my twenty-ninth birthday, I gave birth to a healthy, normal looking baby boy, which we named Braylen. Braylen lived for an hour and a half before passing away in my sister's arms. It took me three years to get to a place where I could talk about him without bursting into tears. Eight years later, I was no longer crying, but I was still keeping his belongings in a storage container in my home. I had been telling myself I was keeping those things in case I had another baby boy, but the reality was that I had not let go of him. That day in September as I realized that this was most likely preventing me from getting pregnant, I went home and began the painful process of preparing his belongings for donation. I cried as I dropped off items that still had tags on them to an unwed teen pregnancy program. Two weeks later, I discovered that I was pregnant and forty weeks later, I gave birth to a healthy baby boy named Jordan. That experience taught me the enormous value letting go of 'things" so that we can move forward in life. A similar thing recently happened to my sister who had been trying to conceive for years without success. Several months ago, she had called to tell me she finally donated clothes and other belongings from a previous relationship to a local charity. A few months later, she discovered that she was pregnant with her first child at the age of 44. As

I write this, she is expecting a healthy baby boy in June of 2017.

Perhaps what happened with my sister and I were coincidences, either way, it cannot hurt to take account of any old wineskins you may have laying around that could be preventing you from the new experiences you wish for and desire.

Clearing Emotional Baggage

Finally, we come to the section on clearing emotional baggage. I covered this topic in the chapter on Bag Ladies, but also wanted to include it in this section as well. As a therapist, I know that it can be scary, intimidating, and emotionally overwhelming to dig up old stuff from the past and acknowledge our emotional wounds, but I have never had one client regret doing their work once the work is completed other than to wish they had done it sooner. The healing journey can be tough, but in the end, it is so worth it. Simply stated, carrying emotional baggage not only ruins romantic relationships, but it also ruins other interpersonal relationships and may ruin your chance at true, authentic happiness. I often use the illustration that it is like wearing dirty, tinted glasses that cause everything we see to appear a certain way. Until we clean the lens and get clear, we may not even realize that our view has been grossly distorted or that we are interpreting our current experiences based on previous ones. Life is too short to keep living in the past, enslaved by old wounds, betrayals, hurts, and disappointments. Give those things a paid in full date, an expiration date and do not waste any more time being angry, vengeful, bitter or resentful towards your parents, siblings, perpetrators, old bosses, and ex-partners. Face it, confront it, own it, and overcome it. If you think surely you will not survive reliving it, keep in mind that if you are here now, then you already survived it at least once.

Chapter 10

Own Your Life

Throughout this book, I have talked about the need to accept and assume responsibility for your relationships, your healing, your happiness, and your life. While I do understand that others may truly be to blame for some of your challenges, issues, problems, and concerns, blaming them does nothing to actually change things or move things forward. Even though it may be tempting to point the finger at your parents, childhood experiences, and certainly the men from your past or present, blaming them will only keep you stuck. That does not mean they are not responsible for the things they have done to you or caused to happen to you, but if you remain stuck, you cannot and will not grow. Ultimately, this will lead to feelings of resentment, bitterness, hatred, and unforgiveness and it may also cause you to build emotional walls that keep people out, but also keep you in. When you hold onto blame and other negative emotions, those emotions have to reside somewhere, and that somewhere is inside of you. There is a book by Dr. Brad Nelson called "The Emotion Code," that explores the concept of trapped emotions and the effects they have on us emotionally, mentally, and even physically. Earlier, I also mentioned the book "Feelings Buried Alive Never Die." Both of these books speak about how buried feelings and emotions can cause us to have emotional challenges like depression and anxiety, and they can also be the underlying causes of physical concerns such as knee pain, allergies, constipation, and more serious conditions like lupus, multiple sclerosis, and cancer. The "Feelings" book even has a section in the back with different physical and emotional conditions and the unresolved or buried feelings related to them.

There is a lot to lose and nothing to be gained by holding onto past hurts and negative emotions. I sometimes work with clients who are still waiting on apologies from someone who wronged them in the past. They simply cannot or will not move forward and start the healing process. Even though they may be justified in their feelings, keeping those feelings is only hurting them and not the perpetrator. One question I always ask is if they are willing to wait forever because the reality is, you cannot control other people and if you need them to acknowledge the wrong and apologize before you can heal and move forward, then you are giving them the power and responsibility for your life. When you accept and own responsibility for your healing, no one else can withhold it from you, take credit for it, or take it away from you.

You also should not resist or prolong your healing process because you are waiting for someone to change. One thing I have learned the hard way is that you can't change other people. It is hard enough trying to change yourself. As I complete this book, we are a few days away from a New Year and lots of people are making New Year's resolutions, plans, and goals for 2017. People will set weight loss goals, fitness goals, health and nutrition goals, financial goals, and educational goals. They will set goals to get organized, stop smoking, meditate, attend church regularly, etc. Sadly, statistics show that only 8% of New Year's resolutions are actually kept and most of them fail within the first week! Change is hard! As a therapist, life coach, speaker, and author, I understand and recognize that I cannot and do not change people. I merely facilitate the process, provide the tools, the information, resources, and feedback, but ultimately it is up to them to change or not to change.

Even though some women blame themselves for their relationship challenges and spend a lot of time judging, criticizing, and beating up on themselves, this too does nothing to usher in the process of change. Again, it keeps you stuck in a place, like the swamp, where nothing is flowing, growing or thriving. Owning your life and accepting responsibility for yourself is not about blaming yourself for the things that have happened to you. In my opinion, self-blame and self-responsibility are two very different things that yield very different results. Self-blame is very negative and self-deprecating. It is finger pointing, fault finding, and assigning a debt that needs to be paid in order to move forward. Self-responsibility on the other hand is a very mature, empowering, life-affirming decision not to judge, criticize, or condemn. It is taking ownership of the life you have been given, the decisions, good and bad; the mistakes, failures, fears, and insecurities. It is owning your stuff so that you can own your relationships and your happiness. It is taking an honest inventory of yourself and making a conscious, mature decision to change what is no longer working or serving you. Self-blame and blaming others is something victims do. Self-responsibility is something overcomers do.

Unfortunately, while some women may blame their relationship challenges on past experiences, others may blame their appearance or the presence or absence of some physical feature such as their skin tone, facial feature, weight, body type, and hair. They may alter those things by losing weight, cutting their hair, adding extensions, working out, bleaching their skin, and undergoing plastic surgery to get liposuction and butt injections, but even though their physical appearance may help them capture the attention of a man, it certainly will not help them keep him. Men are visual beings, and they may appreciate the physical changes and improvements you make, but will you be able to maintain that forever? What will you do when someone comes along who is prettier, younger, and more physically appealing than you? How many surgeries, injections, alterations, pounds lost or pounds gained will ever be enough? I love how TD Jakes phrases it, "It is not about your hips, lips and fingertips." I certainly do not think there is anything wrong with self-improvement. If you desire to lose weight, gain weight, work out, dye your hair, or cut your hair, I feel that is fine, but genuine, lasting attraction goes much deeper than what you see on the surface. Instead of making a lot of expensive, superficial changes to attract a man, concentrate on becoming the woman on the inside who keeps the man. That does not mean you should totally neglect your physical appearance once you have a man because most men do enjoy seeing their women looking nice, but that is not the sole reason he stays in the relationship.

Women may blame their relationship challenges on environmental things such as their geographic location, ethnicity, the prison system, gay men, white women, and a shortage of good Black men. Again, these things may play a role, but they should not determine whether or not you attract and maintain a healthy, loving relationship. Yes, there may be a shortage of good Black men as some of them are already attached or married. I also recognize that there are a lot of Black men locked away in the prison system and for unknown reasons, there is a plentitude of gay Black men, especially in places like Atlanta. Other Black men may exclusively date Caucasian women or women of other races. Have you considered opening yourself up to dating interracially? Have you thought of dating men who are older or younger? Have you thought of relocating? Have you thought of dating outside your normal "type?" I am not saying you have to do any of these things, but your ideal mate may be someone you see and interact with every day but have completely overlooked. Have you made yourself accessible, available, and approachable? Keep in mind, we may not always get to choose the packaging that God sends our ideal mate wrapped in, but that does not take away from the gift that is on the inside. At the end of the day, regardless of who and what may be the blame and the cause of your current or past relationship challenges, it is still your life and it is up to you to make changes if necessary.

Owning your life is not just about accepting and dealing with the bad stuff, it is also being responsible for the really amazing things as well. It is not waiting for a man or anyone else to change you, bring you joy, make you happy, and fill your cup. It is about discovering and walking your own path. If that path requires healing, great. Do the work to bring about healing. If that path requires simply altering the ways you view yourself, men and dating, good, alter it. When all is said and done, take ownership of your life, write your own story and if it is not the way you want it, then make the necessary edits and rewrite it until it becomes your masterpiece!

Chapter 11

Something about Trust

Trust issues. Many of us have dealt with them at some point in our dating lives, so I could not write a book about being single without addressing the topic of trust because I know the power it possesses to destroy even healthy relationships. Trust may be defined as "the firm belief in the reliability, truth, ability or strength of something or someone." Trust begins to form in the first stages of human development. Earlier, I shared Erik Erikson's psychosocial stages of development. The first stage, trust vs. mistrust, begins at birth. This is when infants learn to trust that their caregivers will meet and provide for their basic needs. If their needs are consistently met, trust develops. If they are not met, suspicion, anxiety, and mistrust develop. Even though the foundation of trust begins in infancy, the growth and development of trust do not end there, because while we may start off having our needs consistently met, something could occur to significantly alter that such as the death of a caregiver or other person of significance, parental separation and/or divorce, an accident, sexual or physical abuse, relocation to another area, or any other life altering experience that a person perceives as harmful or traumatic. Regardless of when and how trust issues develop, they can have significant impact on people's lives and their relationships. People who have a difficult time trusting also tend to have issues with safety and security. Insecurity is defined as uncertainty about oneself and a lack of confidence. Synonyms for insecurity include unstable, shaky, unsteady, unsound, flimsy, and unsafe. Unsafety is the state of being open to danger or threat. If you think of a house being built, trust, safety, and security would be the base of the house that comprises the structural foundation. If the structural foundation or base is unstable, shaky, unsteady, flimsy or unsound, essentially the rest of the house will be the same. From what I know about building and construction, everything begins with the foundation. An unstable foundation will eventually cause the entire house to break down, deteriorate, and lose value. Some of the visible signs of foundation problems in a home include cracks in walls or floors, doors and windows that will not open properly, uneven or sloping floors, cracked moldings, etc. No matter how beautiful, spacious, or expensive the final structure may be, an unstable foundation will cause it to be unsteady unless there are major repairs. The same holds true for us. If our caregivers or childhood experiences did not provide us with a strong, steady foundation, we might spend much of our lives looking good on the outside while feeling like a mess on the inside. We will lack confidence, security, and feelings of safety and protection. Not only will we have trust issues in our relationships with others, we are more than likely to also have trust issues with ourselves. The subject of self-trust in my opinion has been seriously overlooked and discounted, and most people have never given it much thought. Typically, when people think of trust or trust issues, they are almost always referring to trusting other people. I believe it is equally if not more important to trust in God and in ourselves. The ability to trust God and ourselves provides the basis for every other relationship or encounter in our lives. Think of the design of a tree. It starts with the base, or trunk, which is rooted in the ground and extends upward towards the sky. While we may only see some of the roots above the ground, a firmly planted tree usually has roots that extend out several feet. Being firmly rooted is what gives the tree its foundation, its sturdiness, and its stability. When opposition comes such as strong winds and rains, the tree may bend, but it rarely breaks. Likewise, our relationship with God and ourselves keeps us firmly planted and rooted when opposition comes our way. I believe this is essential to creating a strong, steady foundation that helps us to feel safe, secure, and able to trust other people. How many times have you failed to trust yourself only to end up regretting it later? Many people get angry at others with whom they have placed their trust if the person ends up betraying them or disappointing them. Then they get angry at themselves because they realize they really failed to trust themselves when they chose to ignore the warning signs that may have been present the entire time. I am not sure why we are taught to trust others without ever being encouraged or taught to also trust ourselves. Perhaps, we think it will cause us to be too self-sufficient or too haughty, but our first relationship should be with ourselves, especially since all our time on earth will be spent with ourselves. Sadly, some people will go their whole lives placing the responsibility of trust in other people and end up being disappointed time and again if and when those expectations are not met. I believe this is why women often overlook warning signs and red flags. We so want to believe in the person or people we have placed our trust in that we negate the need to trust ourselves. Women in general tend to have a very strong sense of intuition, but we are not always good at honoring it and allowing it to guide us and our decisions, especially when it comes to men. Please do not misunderstand me, trusting yourself does not negate or rid you of the need or ability to trust others. In actuality, I believe it provides the basis and foundation that allows you to trust others without completely putting all of your expectations in them to reward and validate your trust.

When my husband and I were dating in the early stages of our relationship, and I was struggling with my own trust issues, I once asked him how he was able to trust me so freely. I knew that I was faithful and truthful, but he had no real way of knowing that. What he said to me forever changed how I view trust. His words were, "I trust you because I trust myself." Deep down inside I realized that I had never learned to trust myself and had always placed other people's words and promises above my own inner knowing. How many times had I known that someone was lying or being untrue to me, yet I believed what they said rather than what I felt and knew or had observed and experienced? I used to say that I trusted people until they gave me a reason not to. I have since learned that trust is something that should not be automatically given, rather it is something that is built and established over time. Remember, the definition of trust is the belief and confidence in the reliability of something or someone. Reliability is established when someone or something continues to be consistent over time. I am not telling you to test people or make them prove themselves in order to gain your trust. I believe that taking the time to get to know someone and building a strong, steady relationship that is consistent and reliable creates the basis and foundation for trust. My longest and most endearing friendships with men and women are those that have been built and developed over time with people who have been consistent and reliable. Even when there have been infractions or indiscretions, we have been able to acknowledge them, confront them, apologize, make amends, and overcome them. The relationships I have had with people that were consistently unreliable, unsteady, and unstable have ended. As I have grown, I am more concerned with the quality of my relationships rather than the quantity of them. Before I began to grow and mature, I would meet people and if I liked their personality or we had similar interests, I would instantly add them to my circle of friends without taking the time to really get to know them or determine if they were worth adding to my circle. Even when I saw warning signs or character flaws, I would often overlook them or justify them by saying, "Everyone has something, including me." Unfortunately, this caused a lot of disappointments, emotional pain, and betrayal. Now, when I meet new people, I do not automatically trust them. I also do not automatically *distrust* them either. Instead, I try to go in with an open mind, willing to ask the tough questions, acknowledge and confront any discrepancies, determine if the relationship serves my best interest and theirs, and cut things off if necessary. This is how I have begun learning to trust myself and to keep my own best interests at heart. This is also what my husband meant.

For those of you with trust issues, learning to trust yourself will be an ongoing process. It will not prevent you from ever being hurt again, nor does it mean you will always be right. Trusting yourself sometimes means being dead wrong about someone or something, but having the courage to honor your truth and go with your own instincts. I think it also means trusting what you will and will not allow. Oftentimes, women do not want to acknowledge and confront the truth and it seems as if sometimes we really do not want to know the truth because knowing might mean we have to act on what we know. So we will trust what a man says rather than trusting what we believe or know to be true. Sometimes we may even want them to be telling the truth so that we can keep things the way they are. I have worked with women who had actual proof of their partner's infidelity, but pretended and chose not to know or act on it because confronting it would mean disrupting the relationship, their homes, and their false sense of security. Isn't it amazing how we will help others make a fool of us at times? Trusting yourself is not an easy task, and if like me, you have had issues with trust, developing it will require the same level of dedication and commitment as building and developing trust in other people. The good thing is when you do begin trusting yourself, you may find that you grow in confidence. You may also find it easier to trust other people because you know what you will and will not allow. Some women do not trust themselves because they do not even know themselves, much less love or like themselves; so the idea of self-trust may be like a foreign language they cannot speak or understand. The good news is that this can change, but it will require you to do the work that is necessary to get to know yourself, honor yourself, like yourself, love yourself, forgive yourself, speak your truth, and own your life. People always say they want to be treated the same way they treat others. I like to add that we should also desire and expect to be treated *by* others the same way we treat ourselves. Remember, we should not expect to receive from someone else what we are not willing to do for and provide to ourselves.

Chapter 12

Let a Man Be a Man

In the first section of this book, I talked about Miss Independent, Superwoman, the concepts of strength and vulnerability and the Black woman's struggle to reconcile one with the other, especially in her interpersonal relationships. In this chapter, I want to touch on this a bit more in detail because I realize the importance of it and its ability to either help our relationships or ruin them. One of the qualities Black women are most known for and most admired for is our strength, yet sometimes our strength is also our greatest downfall. Being strong, independent, or even superwoman is not bad in and of itself. I believe it becomes bad when we allow it to shape and define who we are in a way that almost rejects and detracts from our femininity. Some of us even view our femininity as a weakness, a frailty and an indicator of incompetence, inferiority, or inadequacy. I completely disagree. Perhaps one of the greatest examples of strength and femininity is former first lady, Michelle Obama. Michelle is smart, educated, strong, powerful and independent, yet she is also nurturing, supportive, beautiful, and feminine.

A couple of years ago, I developed a workshop entitled *It is Okay to Be Strong and Feminine*, which is based on this same concept. Being strong should not mean we have to sacrifice our femininity and adopt qualities that are more characteristic of men. I understand that some women have had to play the roles of mother and father out of necessity. My own mother was one of those women and I witnessed firsthand how it hardened her over the years. Being feminine does not mean taking us back to the 1950s or creating a patriarchal power structure that keeps men in control and women subservient. I firmly believe that women are just as smart, capable, and competent as men and there are many things we can do as well as or better than men, but at the end of the day, we are *not* men. We are women, and even the strongest, most independent, competent and capable women in the world will agree that there are distinct differences between us. When I am doing couple's therapy, and one spouse is complaining about how different the other spouse is from them, I remind them that different doesn't mean bad nor is it an indicator of right and wrong. Different is just different. As Black women, we must learn to embrace our feminine selves and understand that this does not mean we are weak or that we are giving men power over us. It means embracing that which makes us unique as women and realizing that it does not diminish nor detract from our strength. Our femininity is one of the biggest things that makes us different from men and attracts them to us. Whenever I speak to women on this issue, I jokingly tell them that a man doesn't want to be in a relationship with another man unless he truly wants another man. Women are able to provide men with something they cannot provide for themselves nor get from other men. Women and men were purposely created and designed with different characteristics, needs, and expectations that are meant to complement one another, not contradict one another or serve as a source of struggle. As strong women, we do not always need to prove ourselves or demonstrate our competence, strength, and independence.

Many of us have become familiar with the concept of the alpha female and I have often encountered them in my professional and my personal life. Women who are educated, high powered, and independent, yet tend to have frequent power struggles with their husbands and significant others because they have not yet learned to blend their strength with their femininity. In some cases where they out earn the man, they have taken on an even more dominant role in their relationships. While their husbands may earn less or be less educated, they are still men who resist and resent the women for attempting to control and dominate the relationship. I make it a point to share with these women a man's need to define and understand his role and purpose in the relationship. Without it, he becomes unsure of himself and may seek out a woman who is nothing like his partner, but a woman who allows him to be the man in her life. Men like and need to feel needed in their relationships. Now, I am not suggesting that strong, independent women should lower themselves in order to please their insecure partners and husbands as I do not believe that this is the definition nor the intention of femininity or submission, but I recognize that men and women have certain emotional needs and if we are unable to get those needs met by our partners, we may be more likely to seek that in others.

Men and women have certain qualities, behaviors, and characteristics that are a natural part of our internal and external makeup. We think differently, feel differently, react differently, smell differently, speak differently, and we place value on different things. The same ways that women tend to value affection and appreciation, men value trust.

Early in my relationship with my husband, we used to argue almost every time we went somewhere due to me complaining that he was driving too fast or following too closely. Sometimes I would grab the dashboard or press my imaginary passenger-side brakes as I tried to prevent us from crashing into the car in front of us. This would often cause heated disagreements between us until one day my husband explained to me how important it was for me to trust him. He shared that it was important for me to trust that he not only knew what he was doing, but that he also had my safety in mind. As a daddy-less daughter, remember I hadn't grown up learning how to trust a man with my safety, but after really listening to how my husband felt, I decided to try it. Instead of me focusing on his driving, I shifted my focus to reading or internet searching to distract myself. Eventually, I began to relax, let go and trust him. While I still might make the occasional comment or press my imaginary brakes, we no longer argue or have disagreements when we travel (by the way, my husband is actually a very safe and cautious driver).

Men and women also differ in our communication. Women love to tell the details of a story while men simply want to know the outcome of the story. Sometimes women may feel dismissed or rejected when men are just being true to their nature. This is when I encourage women to keep a circle of sisters and friends to share those conversations with because other women will appreciate the details of the story and allow you to get it all out. Men simply may not be interested. In Tyler Perry's movie, "Why did I Get Married?", we learned about the 80/20 rule which says that you will not get everything you need from your mate, but you shouldn't sacrifice the 80 you have for the 20 you feel is missing. I know that my husband couldn't care less about some of the topics my girlfriends and I love to discuss. He is unconcerned with the Macy's one day sale, the newest "Housewives" reality show or the latest hairstyle. Likewise, there are conversations he has with his friends that bore me to tears. I have zero interest in knowing about his "lousy fantasy football selection". However, when it comes to the really important things in our relationship such as raising our children, our finances, our marriage, or some physical or emotional concern one of us has, we give that conversation our full attention, time, and respect. I remember when I used to get offended if he showed no interest in what I wanted to discuss, but then I learned not to expect that from him as long as he appreciated things that were most important to me. I decided I would not sacrifice the 80 for the 20.

I could go on and on about the differences between men and women, many of which are obvious, but the purpose of this chapter is to encourage women to allow men to be men and stop feeling threatened by them and stop viewing all men as the enemy. Can some of them act like the enemy or treat you like the enemy? Absolutely. I see that dynamic all the time in couple's therapy. Men and women who profess to love each other, but really view one another as their enemy. Men and women who have built up so much resentment, hostility, and contempt towards one another before they decide to seek counseling as a last resort. I see men who do not know how to really love their wives or what it means to be the head of their households, and don't understand how necessary and relevant they are to the viability of the marriage and the family. I see women with something to prove, who refuse to submit to their husbands because they see submission as weak and subservient. As a result, their marriages and relationships are out of order and headed towards separation and divorce.

At one time in my life, I struggled with this as well because I used to see men as the enemy and I was never going to submit to them. One day, a very wise older married woman shared something with me. She said, "Men are the head of the household." As soon as she said it, I believe she could hear me about to object, and she "shushed" me. She went on to say, "But a woman is the neck and the head can't do anything without the neck." All of a sudden, I got it! I am not sure why that simple illustration was so profound and helpful for me, but all I know is that I began to view the dynamics between men and women very differently and from that moment on, I no longer saw men as the enemy, and I no longer saw myself as having something to prove. I learned that when it is the right man, it won't even feel like submitting, and you will naturally allow him to lead and guide you. I also learned that submission is built on trust. I believe you have to trust someone in order to submit yourself to them. I do not just mean trusting him not to cheat on you, but trusting that he truly cares for you and has your best interest at heart; also trusting and allowing him to protect and cover you. With all the things we face in the world, having someone to cover us as women is an amazing demonstration of love and respect. It is also what a good father provides for us as children. A good man will even cover our sins, our mistakes, our past, our fears, and our insecurities. I know it was because of my husband and him covering me that I was able to heal from my past hurts and emotional wounds and even write this book exposing some of my innermost secrets to the world. My husband, who I affectionately refer to as my Mufasa from the Lion King, covered me and gave me the space, the security, the acceptance, and the love that I needed to face the giants in my life and slay them. But if I had continued see him as an enemy, he would have viewed me and treated me as an enemy and not the woman he desires to love and protect. Whenever I speak to marriage groups on this, I always discuss the importance of men and women seeing one another as allies instead of adversaries. Think about it. An adversary is someone you want to win *against* and an ally is someone you want to win *with*.

In closing, I understand that some men have done things to cause women to lose trust and see them as the enemy, but if you are going to stay with him and make things work, you have to find a way to get over the hurt, forgive him, and move on. Otherwise, why bother? Why stay in the relationship and continue to build more contempt and hostility… each day, chipping away a little more at one another until there is nothing left? Life is too short. Either forgive and move on or end it and move on. Either way, move on.

Chapter 13

Becoming Clear About What You Want

I once had a newly divorced client who was looking to start dating again. This client was considering paying thousands of dollars for an online relationship course that was designed to help people identify what they wanted in a partner. When she asked my advice on whether she should sign up for the course, I suggested that she think about what she no longer wanted based on her previous marriage and then create a list of the attributes she desired to have in her next relationship. I also recommended that she complete a vision board for our next session and I advised her to be specific without being superficial. For example, it is perfectly okay to desire a partner who shares your spiritual beliefs, but it may be superficial to want someone with hazel eyes. This may be a preference, but not necessarily a must have or a deal breaker. A few months later, my client came in excited to tell me she had met someone with whom she felt an instant connection. I advised her to take things slowly and really get to know him since instant connections can sometimes be misleading. I reminded her to be determined to see the truth, acknowledge it, and walk in it to avoid having to face it and confront it later down the line. My client is currently still in her new relationship although she readily admits they are past the honeymoon stage which is a natural progression in most relationships. We meet people with whom we may or may not have an instant connection and then months later, we begin to see them for their true selves instead of their "relationship representatives." If you recall, I, along with Steve Harvey and Joan Clayton from Girlfriends, suggest that you spend at least 90 days getting to know someone before you decide to take things to the next level. If you are a believer, you may decide to wait until you are married. The truth is, it is okay to be giddy. It is okay to have butterflies in your stomach. It is okay to be excited. Just remember that those are all emotions, and emotions can and do change over time. Not that it means they will change into something bad or harmful, but things will become more "real." That awesomely wonderful person who was so perfect in the beginning will begin to show you their flaws just as they will start to see your flaws. Seeing these flaws before you get in too deep, have sex, or make any other serious commitments will help you to make more rational decisions. Making life changing decisions based on short term emotions can be detrimental, foolish, and heartbreaking. Please know that it is okay to take care of yourself, to trust yourself, and to keep your best interests at heart. Genuine intimacy, trust and reliability rarely happen instantly. Instead, they are built and established over time. Believe me, I have been there myself a time or two, but only when I decided to do things differently did it result in a different outcome. I took that 90 days to get to know my husband and to allow him to get to know me. From all of my failed past relationships, I knew exactly what I did not want and I knew exactly what I did want based on my preferences, my personality, my belief system, my values, and the vision I had for my life. I wrote my list long before I met my husband and I was specific, but not superficial. I wrote down that I wanted someone who was not only financially stable, but would also share his finances to provide for the family and me, because some men may be financially stable, but they may also be selfish with their money. What I did not write down was someone with long eyelashes and wavy hair. Not that there is anything wrong with preferences because it is important to be physically and sexually attracted to your mate, especially if you intend to settle down with them, but remember not to get caught up and distracted by the superficial and overlook the man's character. I know far too many women who have gotten caught up in status, material items, and looks while overlooking and excusing serious character flaws. Remember the narcissist? He may be that guy who looks great on paper, but is he what you desire in a husband and father/stepfather for your children? Is he the guy who will hold your hand and let you cry on his shoulder when you suffer a loss or disappointment in your life?

I regularly advise women in my personal and professional capacity to always look at character. Character is defined as the mental and moral qualities of an individual, but my definition of character goes a step further. To me, character is similar to integrity, and it refers to a person being true to who they are regardless of external factors. For example, if a man does not acknowledge and support his other children, why should you be surprised if he refuses to acknowledge and provide support for yours? If he stole money from his last partner, why would you lend him your credit card and then get outraged when he steals from you? If he cheated on his wife or girlfriend WITH you, why would you expect him not to cheat ON you? Character speaks volumes. Conversely, if he is good to his mother, his sisters, and other women in his life, it is a good sign he will also be good to you. If he is generally a respectful person to his friends, neighbors, and colleagues, then chances are he will be respectful to you. One of the greatest character traits I noticed early in my husband is that he would not only hold the door open for me to walk through, but he would also hold it open for other women as well.

When observing a man's character, take notice of the types of friends he has, what he values, how he spends his money and his time, and his views on relationships, marriage, and family because these things all define and depict character. Listen to what he says, but also watch what he does. Are his actions congruent with his words? Does he practice what he preaches or is he just pretending and trying to impress you? This is why it is good to give a relationship time to grow and develop because during that time, you will most likely be able to observe and take notice of these things. When you do see discrepancies, call them to his attention. Not in an accusatory way, but bring it up in a discussion and give him the opportunity to explain. If the explanation is plausible and believable, then make a decision as to whether you believe it, but continue to be vigilant and watch for other signs of incongruence. Again, people will only be able to hide who they really are but for so long. Eventually, just as with the house with foundation problems, the cracks will begin to show and the relationship will become unsteady, unstable, and unreliable.

Another thing to consider in regards to character and values is how well he balances and prioritizes things in his life. We all want a man who works hard and provides, but be careful that he doesn't value his work, his career, and his money above everything else because you will be the one sitting at home alone while he is still at work, and going to your children's activities unaccompanied while he is in a meeting or on a business trip. Likewise, we want a guy who is likable, social and has friends, but does he value those friends above his woman or does he prioritize your relationship and create a healthy balance between you? The truth is that some men may start out spending all their time with you at the beginning of the relationship while he is pursuing you, but once the newness begins to wear off and the thrill of the chase is gone, he will most likely return to spending ample time with his friends and other interests. Also, be aware of the type of friends he keeps. Are they all single men who have no desire to settle down and get married? Are they married men who readily cheat on their wives? If either is true, it is not your job to try and change him or change his friends as most men will resist this and may even resent you. It is your job to be aware of what you may be walking into or dealing with so that you can make a decision as to whether this is something you want to endure. As much as we need to know what we want and what we do not want, we also need to understand and know what we can and cannot endure. Self-awareness and self-trust again are crucial. Knowing yourself and knowing what you can truly live with is essential to having a healthy, lasting relationship. For me, I cannot live with an abuser, drug addict, criminal or narcissist. I have dated a couple in my past, so I know what I do not want and what does not work for me. Once I learned to truly like and trust myself, I was able to set boundaries in my relationships, and I became confident in establishing what I would no longer tolerate and allow. Now I jokingly tell my husband that if we ever separate, I pity the next guy because my husband has set the bar so high that I cannot imagine going back to the mess I tolerated before him. My husband is a good man, but he is certainly not perfect, and neither am I. We both decided early on that we could endure each other's flaws and shortcomings. I don't care who you are, you will always have to overcome something in your relationship, so give up the search for the perfect man because he does not exist any more than you exist as the perfect woman, but he may be perfect for you. In order to discover who is perfect for you, you will actually have to get to know yourself and have the courage to wait for the right guy, believing that you are worth it. Don't find and date just any guy and try to make him the right guy because even if he seems right, he may not be right for you. There are many good men out there who may not be *your* good man. Sadly, some women will desire and pursue another woman's husband or significant other because she foolishly believes that if he is good to his wife or partner, he will also be good to her. The truth is that a man who is good to someone else may be horrible to you and for you, so you should never covet someone else's life, their relationship or their blessings because the things that have been designed and designated for them might make you miserable. The universe is abundant, and there are enough men to go around, so make the choice to trust God and yourself to meet and connect with your own good man and not someone else's. Not only are you likely to end up with your heart broken, you will activate the law of sowing and reaping so that if and when you do meet and marry your Boaz, don't be surprised if that is exactly when your karma decides to show up and you begin to reap the discord you have sown into another woman's life. All actions have consequences, and as adults, we are responsible for the choices we make and the consequences that follow. I understand you may genuinely develop feelings for someone who is in a relationship and I believe you cannot always control what you feel; however, you can control what you do with those feelings. A good thing to ask yourself is this, "If this were my man, would I be okay with it?" If the answer is no, then step back, and respect and honor yourself. There may also be a situation where you meet someone who claims to be single only to discover later that he is married or living with someone, which is yet one more reason it is important to take your time to get to know someone so that you can watch for evidence of his honesty, reliability, and character. Does he disappear at night or on holidays? Does he turn his phone off at certain times of day? Have you been to his home? Ask yourself and him the tough questions, especially if you begin to see discrepancies. After all, it is your life, and it is up to you to take good care of your heart and your interests. Proverbs 4:23 reminds us, "Above all else, guard your heart for everything you do flows from it."

Another translation says, "Guard your heart above all else for it determines the course of your life." Guarding our hearts is not the same as keeping our hearts behind emotional walls, rather it means protecting your heart, "for out of it flow the issues of life."

Once you begin to get clear in knowing who and what you want, then you have to have the ability to actually recognize when your potential mate has shown up. Whenever I work with clients in this area, I always assign them the task of determining how they will know by comparing it to a favorable experience. One of my favorite things to do is take a hot, relaxing bubble bath with scented candles, music and maybe even a glass of sweet red wine. The best part for me is that first moment when I slide into the water and feel all my cares begin to float away as the hot water surrounds me and embraces me with its warmth causing me to feel safe, protected, and accepted. Several years ago, I decided this was how I wanted to feel with my future husband. Not as a one-time event or a hit or miss type of thing or with someone else's man, but as an ongoing theme in our relationship. This may sound silly or unnecessary, but some women have been so abused, mistreated, deceived, and disrespected that they are unable to recognize a good man or a healthy relationship when it shows up. Identifying the way you wish to feel could help provide a reference point. Using a metaphor just makes it more fun. If you expect to feel safe and protected in your relationship and all you feel is emotional turmoil and insecurity, then that may indicate the need to re-evaluate. If you desire and expect to feel loved and accepted as you are, yet you always feel the need to change in order to please him; that is another indicator that something may be off. I cannot stress enough the need to do your inner work so that you can go into a relationship whole and complete rather than lacking and needy so you can attract, recognize, and accept a healthy relationship if and when it shows up. Have you ever sabotaged a good relationship because of past experiences, fears, and insecurities? Have you ever rejected someone before he could reject you even if you felt he may be a keeper or at least worth getting to know better? Have you ever mistreated a man you knew would make a good father and husband because he seemed too nice or too safe? Remember, we are all acting out our dramas in life, and until we get clear, the same story lines and themes will continue to show up and play themselves out. We attract who we are, so do your work so that you can be clear about who and what you want, what is best for you and what you deserve, and then trust God and have faith in your ability to attract and maintain your divine equivalent.

You also may have to make room in your life for your divine right mate to show up. According to prosperity teachings, the universe hates a vacuum which is defined as an empty or available space. This is based on the belief that if we create and provide an available space to be filled, the universe will send someone or something to fill it. Prior to purchasing my first home, I read a book on the Chinese philosophy called Feng Shui. This particular book on Feng Shui focused on relationships, and it stated that if you desire to be in a relationship, you should create a space for it in your home and your life. It also recommended simple, practical things you should do like buying two nightstands for your bedroom or setting an extra place at the dinner table. Regardless of whether there was any truth to it or not, I decided to purchase two nightstands when I bought my bedroom set, and I placed them in the four bedroom house I purchased while it was still just me and my shih-tzu puppy, Bella. I remember one of my cousins asking me why I had bought such a big house and why I bought two nightstands when it was just me. I explained to her that it was because I did not want it to always be "just me". I was creating a vacuum. Now ten years later, when I look over at my handsome husband laying on his side of the bed reading from the lamp sitting on *his* nightstand while our two children sleep in their own separate bedrooms down the hall, I am glad I followed this simple advice and that it is no longer just me. I created a space, and the universe filled it. Actually, we have now outgrown this home, and are in the process of planning our next move.

Finally, in becoming clear about what you want in a man, you have to know what you are worth and what you deserve which means you may have to be alone or "all one" for a while. When you do meet someone who seems to be the right one, give it time. Get to know him, look at his character and integrity, and always trust yourself.

In my pastor's relationship series "What Makes a Woman," he shared a story about how a female eagle chooses her mate. She doesn't simply accept the first proposal from a potential male prospect. Instead, she puts him through some tests. The first test is when she flies to a high ledge and drops a stick to see if he will catch it before it hits the ground. If he succeeds in the first test, she then flies to a higher ledge and repeats this same test several times, each time checking to see if he will catch the stick. The final test is when she flies to the highest ledge she can find, and she allows herself to fall from the ledge to see if he will catch her before "she" hits the ground. If he is able to pass each of these tests, he is selected as her mate. Like the female eagle, I believe women should also be willing to make sure a potential mate can and will "catch" her in life in order to determine if he is the one.

Chapter 14

The Point of it All

Although the research article that inspired me to write this book almost eight years ago was about the Black woman's unlikely chances of getting married, *Why Am I Still Single* is about so much more than that. Hopefully, you have begun to see that as you made your way through each chapter and arrived here for these final words. My prayer is for women to put this book down and walk away with life changing, eye opening information and insight that will not only transform their relationships, but also change the ways they see men, love, life, and themselves. I also hope that women will refer to it often as their relationship journeys continue and progress. This was never meant to be a how-to guide. Later this year, I intend to release a workbook that will include practical tips and techniques to assist you with emotional healing, clearing clutter, breaking soul ties, and more.

From beginning to the end, the goal and purpose of this book has been to help you discover and acknowledge the truth about yourself in a loving, forgiving, compassionate way; to learn to honor and respect yourself; trust God and trust yourself; fill your own cup from the inside out; and to grow in self-awareness, self-worth, self-acceptance, self-discovery, and self-love. Every relationship we have flows out of the one we have with ourselves. If our relationships with others are broken, then it is essential that we examine the relationship we have with us. While on the surface, we may appear to have it all together, many of us are still wounded little girls who require healing of the heart, mind, body, and soul. Others of us are big girls who seem to have all the right ingredients, yet still cannot attract and maintain a healthy, loving relationship.

If you are already married, engaged or otherwise attached, but struggling in those relationships and asking yourself if it is worth it to stay or wondering why things are so hard, my prayer is that this book will only serve to strengthen those relationships with the men in your life as you heal and strengthen the relationship you have with yourself. If you are divorced, separated or on the verge of trying it again, I hope this book provides you with something that may help you identify what may have gone wrong previously and what may need to be changed or adjusted moving forward. If you have given up on love because you have tried and failed, please don't lose hope. Ultimately, loving yourself is all that really matters. When you learn to truly love, value, like, and appreciate yourself, you are never alone even if you sometimes feel lonely.

For my single girls who still believe, still have hope, and are still seeking, please use what you have gained and learned in this book as you go out into the dating world and do not feel pressured to compromise your values, your worth, your integrity or your virtue for something that hasn't proven itself to be real. Keep in mind that heartbreak is not 100% preventable for anyone. When you love someone and give them your heart, you are taking a risk. We all do. But it is so worth it. Guard your heart. Protect it, but do not hide it. The heart was made to love. There are never any guarantees in life or in love, but having the courage and the willingness to try is so much more exciting than sitting on the sidelines. I will leave you with this. The players sitting on the sidelines of life are watching the game of life and love being played without actually being in it. The players on the field may run the risk of being bruised, trampled on, and wounded. Sadly though, so do the players on the sidelines. Think about it, haven't you still been hurt by someone or something even though you have tried to stay on the sidelines and have hidden your heart behind emotional walls? Sure you have. We all have. Hurt and pain are universal. So if you stand the chance of getting hurt either way, why not at least get hurt being in the game rather than watching from the sidelines because one thing is for certain, no one ever shot a winning basket, ran a touchdown or hit a homerun from the sidelines.

It has taken me many years to learn and unlearn who I was, who I wasn't and really begin to understand and acknowledge my own personal need to accept responsibility for my own life. One of the hardest things for me to do was to remove the mask I had been wearing, show people my scars, and allow them to see me and all of my stuff. I also had to develop the courage to expose the false self I had created and become and reveal my genuine, authentic self. Writing this book has allowed me another opportunity to do just that. I have shown you my scars, removed my mask, and revealed myself to many in hopes that my story, my life, my knowledge, and my wisdom will help women around the world to find the courage to heal and live their lives with purpose, passion, faith, trust, hope, boundaries, wisdom, forgiveness, love, and authenticity.

Until next time…….

Made in the USA
Columbia, SC
10 March 2018